Plan & Go | John Muir Trail

All you need to know to complete one of the world's greatest trails

Gerret Kalkoffen, Kevin Muschter

sandiburg press

Plan & Go | John Muir Trail

All you need to know to complete one of the world's greatest trails

ISBN 978-1-943126-05-7

Published by sandiburg press
www.sandiburgpress.com

Cover photos: South of Mather Pass (front); Evolution Valley (back)

Safety Notice: This book describes physically challenging activities in remote outdoor environments which carry an inherent risk of personal injury or death. While the author(s) and sandiburg press have made every effort to ensure that the information contained herein was accurate at the time of publication, they are not liable for any damage, injury, loss, or inconvenience arising directly or indirectly from using this book. Your safety and health during preparations and on the trail are your responsibility. This book does not imply that any of the trails described herein are appropriate for you. Make sure you fully understand the risks, know your own limitations, and always check trail conditions as they can change quickly.

Content

Welcome

This book was written to provide all the necessary information to help you thoroughly prepare and successfully complete a hike on the John Muir Trail (JMT). Regardless of whether you intend to walk America's most famous wilderness path from end to end or in sections, I am confident you will be well-equipped and save valuable time and effort on planning if you use the information and advice compiled in this guide.

The book's title is a reference to my approach to anything. I find it best to put generous thought into how I want to do something, then plan and organize, and ultimately get going. The following chapters provide the most relevant information for planning and preparing a hike on the JMT in a short but comprehensive manner. The book also touches on the history of the trail and the flora and fauna encountered, with references to more comprehensive resources on these subjects. No matter whether you are still toying with the idea of hiking the JMT or have already decided to embark on this adventure, I hope this book will be a helpful guide and source of inspiration – both for less experienced and advanced hikers.

The setting of the JMT in the California High Sierra Mountains is breath-taking. Each day, you will experience new landscapes: lush meadows with grazing deer, clear streams babbling amidst dark pine forests, or nothing but sunburnt rocks and boulders. Throughout a long summer stretch, weather conditions will be very pleasant. It is absolutely worth taking a few weeks off to experience the solitude and nature's beauty along the trail. I promise, completing the JMT will be one of the greatest and most memorable experiences of your life.

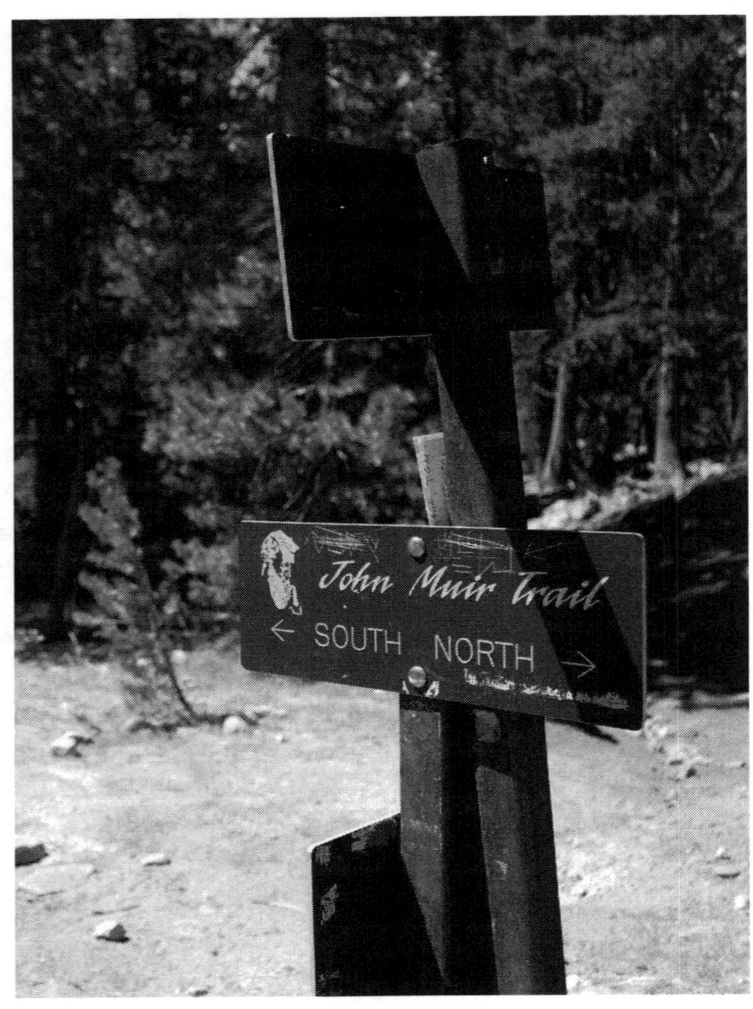

JMT Waymarker near Le Conte Ranger Station

1. Introduction

The Sierra Nevada, also known as High Sierra or the Sierras, is a mountain range in the Western United States, stretching 400 miles (644km) from north to south and roughly 70 miles (113km) across from east to west. The vast majority of the range lies in the state of California, with only a small area reaching into the neighboring state of Nevada. Known for its imposing granite peaks and expansive glacially-carved valleys, the High Sierra is rich in natural and geological features, which attract millions of outdoor enthusiast from all over the world each year.

Located in the southern half of the Sierras, the John Muir Trail runs 211 miles (340km) in north-to-south direction from Yosemite Valley in Yosemite National Park to the summit of the highest mountain in the contiguous United States, 14,505-foot (4,421m) Mt. Whitney. Leading through three national parks, two wilderness areas, and one national monument, this multi-week journey abounds with picturesque landscapes and most spectacular sceneries of canyons, cliffs, forests, lakes, rivers, peaks, and passes of over 14,000 feet (4,270m). It is for these reasons that the JMT is one of the most renowned trails in the world and repeatedly recognized as one of the greatest long-distance treks of our time.

The John Muir Trail, as we know it today, was planned and constructed over several decades in the early to mid-1900s. The original idea of establishing a route along the crest of the Sierra Nevada is attributed to the explorer and early member of the Sierra Club, Theodore Solomons. Based on his advocacy, other Sierra Club members ventured into the Sierras to explore possible routes and, eventually, a collaboration was formed between the club and the state of California to commence the construction of the trail. It took many years to blaze the path through rough terrain and, ultimately, required the joint efforts of Forest Service and National Park Service to complete the enormous undertaking in 1938.

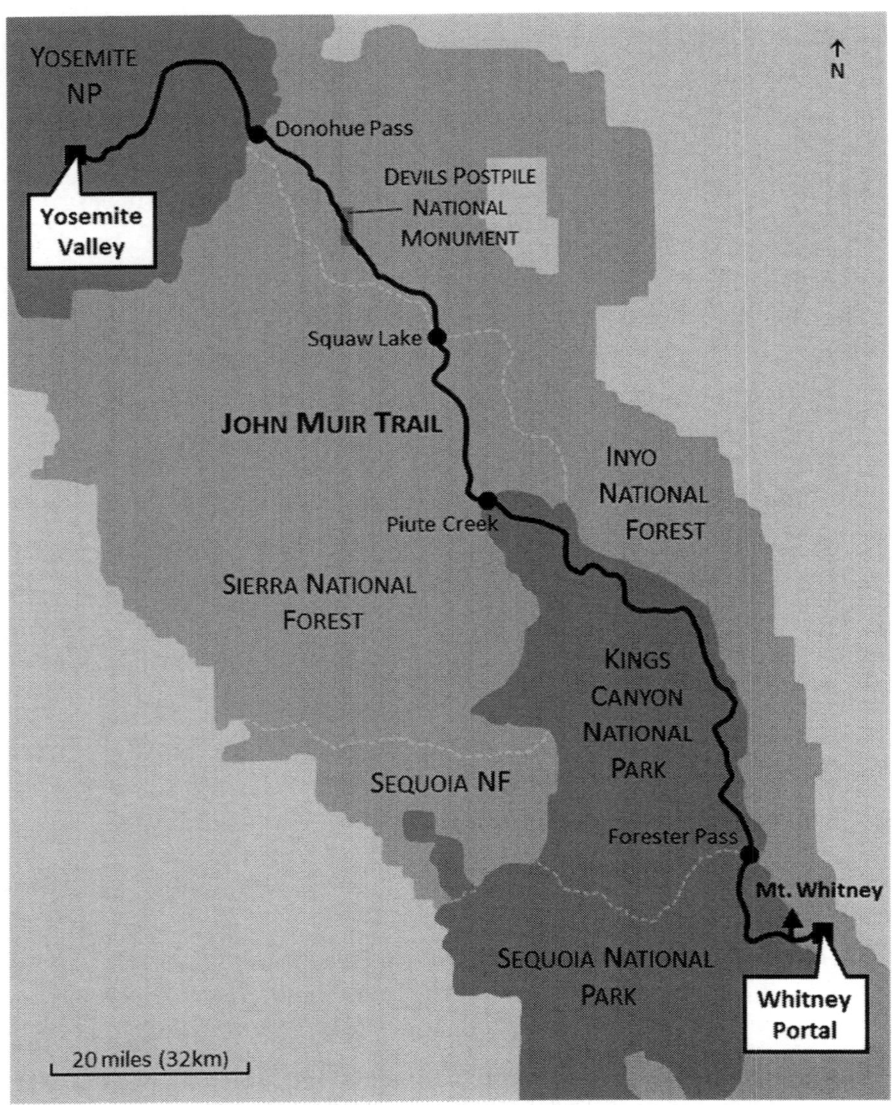

Figure 1 – Overview Map of the John Muir Trail

Originally called High Sierra Trail, the name was later changed in honor of John Muir, the Scottish-American naturalist, author, and founder of the Sierra Club. During his lifetime, John Muir explored the Sierra Nevada like no other and documented his inspirational journeys in numerous letters, essays, and books. Driven by his boundless appreciation of the natural world, he became one of the early advocates of wilderness preservation in the U.S. Through his tireless activism and inspirational writings, "John of the Mountains" enthused millions of individuals, including leading legislators, which eventually led to the establishment of national parks.

My personal JMT journey came about just after I had moved to San Diego, California, a few years back. With a vague idea of wanting to switch careers, I had some time to spare when one of my best friends, Josh, who was on a one-year sabbatical and looking for an adventure, called me one day and asked if I had heard of the JMT. Unfamiliar with trail, I said no but looked into it and was immediately stunned. Though I love hiking, I had never camped for more than three days in a row, let alone planned and prepared a backpacking trip of this magnitude. Nevertheless, my initial concerns were put on hold when I saw pictures of this exceptional trail.

After talking with Josh so more, we decided to go for it. I bought a book, studied lots of blogs, several online forums, and the National Parks' websites and soon learned that getting a wilderness permit would be the bottleneck. As I continued my research, my confidence grew. I found that the JMT would be the perfect amount of adventure: located in remote wilderness areas, sporadically frequented by other hikers, a few ranger stations, and several exit points to nearby towns. The more sources I combined, the better my picture of the JMT became and the more capable I felt of the challenge. At the end, we finished the trail in 15 days and, to this day, it remains the most memorable backpacking experience of my life.

The first edition of this guidebook, published in 2014, was a comprehensive summary of all the knowledge and advice I had gathered during my own research and preparations. It also contained many valuable lessons that we learned ourselves out on the trail and that were shared with us by fellow JMT'ers we met along the way. For this edition, we have broadened the scope to better address the major challenges resulting from the JMT's ever-increasing popularity. You will find a more extensive overview of alternate entry points, required permits, and most successful permit application strategies. For those who wish to hike only a portion of the trail, we have also compiled an overview of popular JMT section hikes that can be completed in a week or less. Last but not least, we have reviewed and updated all facts and figures to provide the most current planning information possible.

The following chapters will provide a clear picture of what to expect on the JMT and how to best prepare yourself. *Chapter 2* summarizes the challenge at hand in terms of physical and technical requirements. It also provides tools to estimate the time and budget needed. *Chapter 3* gives an overview of trail and weather conditions, points of interest along the route, camping options, water availability, notes on safety, as well as animal and plant life. *Chapter 4* discusses trip planning items that require sufficient lead time, such as permit applications and travel arrangements. *Chapter 5* covers specific details on itinerary planning, proper training, and nutrition to help you carefully and effectively prepare your own trip. *Chapter 6* provides an overview of essential hiking gear items needed together with JMT-specific advice and recommendations. Lastly, *Chapter 7* summarizes all efforts and considerations that went into our own 15-day JMT adventure, along with a day-by-day account and many anecdotes.

We hope you will find all the information you need in this guide to feel more confident and prepared to hike the JMT.

Happy Trails!

Visit *www.PlanAndGoHiking.com* for more information and pictures.

2. Summary of the Challenge

Can you hike the John Muir Trail? If you are keen on hiking in pristine alpine wilderness and have already gained some experience with overnight backpacking, then the answer is most likely YES. Completing the 221 miles (356km), including 47,800 feet (14,600m) in elevation gain and 43,200 feet (13,200m) in elevation loss, is a challenge that will put your physical endurance and mental fortitude to the test. However, with the right preparation and a positive mindset, the JMT embodies a rewarding adventure that is more than achievable!

a. Requirements

The general requirements for hiking the JMT include surefootedness in varying terrain, the ability to deal with high altitudes and changing weather conditions, as well as a good level of overall fitness. For the most part, the JMT is a well-maintained path in order to allow for access by pack animals. It is a non-technical trail, which means no climbing skills and gear are required. However, if you intend to hike during a time when snowy conditions are to be expected, typically from late fall to late spring, special gear and skills are necessary to ensure a safe journey. During the summer months, be prepared to get your feet wet while crossing some of the streams that intersect the path. Depending on the availability of water in the High Sierra from snowmelt/rain, it may even be necessary to wade through knee-deep rivers in order to continue your trek.

From an individual perspective, a strong back and knees will be required to carry the weight of your gear and supplies. Depending on your packing preferences, this could amount to 30-45 lbs. (14-20kg). Be prepared to deal with significant swings between daytime (very hot) and nighttime (near/below freezing) temperatures. Since camping is the only option for accommodation (with very few exceptions), you must be able to set up your own shelter, know how to prepare your meals with limited resources, and be comfortable answering nature's call in the wild.

b. Time

The average time needed to walk the distance between Yosemite Valley and Whitney Portal is 16-22 days. Hikers may decide on a more ambitious or a more leisurely itinerary depending on their personal hiking goals, the available time, and their overall experience and fitness. Given the spectacular scenery along the trail, choosing a more relaxed pace is certainly recommended. However, in times where speed hiking and trail running are becoming increasingly popular, individual motives may differ.

FYI: While this guide's primary goal is to promote the recreational aspects of hiking the JMT, you may find it interesting to know that, at present, the fastest known times for completing the full distance between Whitney Portal and Happy Isles on foot are 3 days 7 hours 36 minutes (supported attempt by Leor Pantilat in 2014) and 3 days 10 hours 59 minutes 40 seconds (unsupported attempt by Andrew Bentz in 2014).

Now back to reality. In order to have an enjoyable experience with an adequate challenge, start by estimating your days on the trail. Your estimate of trail days (ETD) will help with all of your further planning, especially regarding your permit, travel, food, and resupply. Figure 2 below is intended to provide guidance for an initial assessment.

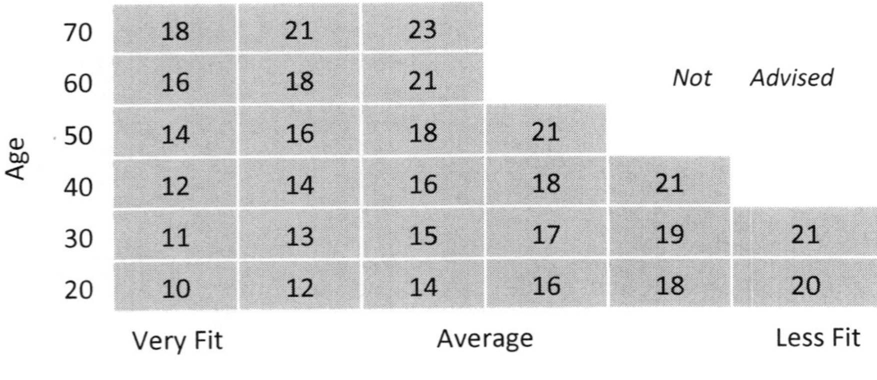

Age	Very Fit		Average			Less Fit
70	18	21	23			
60	16	18	21		*Not*	*Advised*
50	14	16	18	21		
40	12	14	16	18	21	
30	11	13	15	17	19	21
20	10	12	14	16	18	20

Level of Fitness

Figure 2 – Estimate of Trail Days (ETD)

Selecting your age and corresponding fitness level will give you an idea of how long it will approximately take you to complete the trail. For example, a 40-year-old person of average fitness can expect to take roughly 16-18 days to complete the JMT, so let's assume 17. Once you have determined your ETD, you can calculate your average daily mileage by dividing the total distance of the JMT by your ETD:

Average miles per day = 221 miles / ETD

Continuing the above example leads to 221/17 = 13 miles per day on average. While this is a good initial estimate, additional factors need to be taken into consideration as they will impact actual daily distances and, thus, the overall duration of your hike. These include:

- Total weight of gear and food (heavier packs cause earlier fatigue)
- Resupply strategy (additional time spend off-trail to pick up supplies)
- Frequency and duration of stops (e.g., for taking photos, appreciating scenery, relaxing)
- Difficulty of a particular trail section (i.e., elevation gain/loss)
- Taking rest days, going for a swim, washing clothes, etc.
- Extra time needed for taking side trips

During my own 15-day trek on the JMT, I met a 74-year-old who had budgeted 24 days with his wife; a 67-year-old who was doing the JMT in 32 days (for the 8th time!); a 63-year-old who finished in 16 days, and a 50-year-old who completed the trail in 15 days as well.

c. Budget

Walking the John Muir Trail is quite affordable for the most part. At present, advance permit reservation fees range between $10-20 per person for the entire duration of the hike. Walk-up permits are free of charge and so is wild camping along the trail. If you would like to incorporate a few comforts by staying at one of the more established campgrounds, you can expect to spend between $6 and $22 per night, depending on the amenities offered.

Getting to and from the trail will likely represent the largest portion of the required budget, unless you are fortunate enough to live close by. Related expenses may include airfare to one of the nearby hub cities, gas money and long-term parking fees if you decide to drive, cost of accommodation at the beginning and end of your trip, as well as expenses for public transportation and/or private shuttles to get to and from the trailheads.

You will also need to factor in expenses for the food and fuel you will consume during your trip and the cost of mailing your resupply packages to the respective locations. If you don't currently own all the required gear for backpacking the JMT or need to upgrade a few items, you will want to budget for those expenses well. Given the demanding nature of this 221-mile trip, it is highly recommended to opt for good quality equipment that is not only functional and durable but also as comfortable and lightweight as possible.

* * *

Figure 3 – Half Dome and Nevada Fall in Yosemite Valley

3. What to Expect

The John Muir Trail is a wonderful, highly rewarding physical challenge, offering striking mountain scenery, exciting wildlife encounters, and a memorable backpacking experience that can rival anywhere in the world. This chapter is intended to give you an impression of the conditions and highlights along the route. You will get a clear picture of what to look forward to and what to look out for when attempting to thru-hike this trail. The information provided will also assist you in choosing appropriate gear and setting realistic expectations.

a. Trails & Navigation

The official length of the JMT, as stated by the United States Geological Survey (USGS), is 210.4 miles (338.6 km) from its northern terminus at Happy Isles in Yosemite Valley to its southern terminus at the top of Mt. Whitney. Since it is not really possible to end your journey at the 14,505-foot peak, you will have to walk an additional 10.7 miles to the nearest trailhead at Whitney Portal, resulting in a combined total distance of 221.1 miles.

Hiking Direction

The JMT can be hiked in both north-to-south and south-to-north direction. Even modified itineraries, starting somewhere in the middle, are possible. Below are a few pointers, outlining the pros and cons of each option:

North to South (also: southbound or "SOBO"):

- By far the most popular route
- Since the vast majority of hikers walks in the same direction, you encounter fewer people on the trail
- You avoid the Mt. Whitney permit lottery
- The scenery gets more dramatic as you go
- You gradually acclimate to higher altitudes before reaching Mt. Whitney

- Uphill sections are mostly north-facing and will be more forested and shaded
- You can opt to start lighter by taking advantage of the shorter distances between resupply stations early on the trail

South to North (also: northbound or "NOBO"):

- The sun mostly hits your back rather than your face when hiking up tough passes
- You get to hike with Pacific Crest Trail hikers
- It is generally downhill hiking towards the end of the trip
- Transportation upon arrival in Yosemite is easier
- Given the risk of an unintended early exit, you saw the monumental Mt. Whitney

Starting in the Middle (also: modified or "MOBO"):

In recent years, a third, less conventional option has gained more attention as a result of the increased demand for SOBO and NOBO permits. A MOBO hiker starts the trail in the middle, hikes either north to Happy Isles or south to Mt. Whitney, then returns to the middle and completes the remaining portion of the trail in the opposite direction (also known as 'flip-flop'). Permits for this option are easier to get than starting in Yosemite Valley or at Whitney Portal.

Trail Conditions

The JMT is mostly a somewhat narrow, single-lane trail that feels like a minimal disruption to the surrounding wilderness. As the path is also frequented by horses and mules (although rarely), there is never a need for climbing involving your hands. However, there are very steep, winding sections with sudden drop-offs to the sides, where you wonder how these large animals can make it. The drop-offs and ledges also call for you to be fairly comfortable with heights.

The predominant surfaces you will walk on are well-compacted dirt, gravel, and rock. However, the rock can vary from large slabs of immovable granite or basalt, to loosely touching small boulders that shift under your feet. Loose gravel or even sand and dust, on the other hand, may provide soft resistance as you push forward. Consequently, conditions on the trail can range from dry and dusty, to slippery when wet or muddy. Surefootedness is a must.

The slope of the trail is usually anything but flat. Switchbacks and steps are utilized liberally to help you make the numerous ascents and descents. You will cross a total of 10 named mountain passes, and there are several sections where big elevation gains or losses occur within a single day *and* over a relatively short distance. To help you plan for these physically taxing events, Figure 4 below shows an elevation profile of the trail.

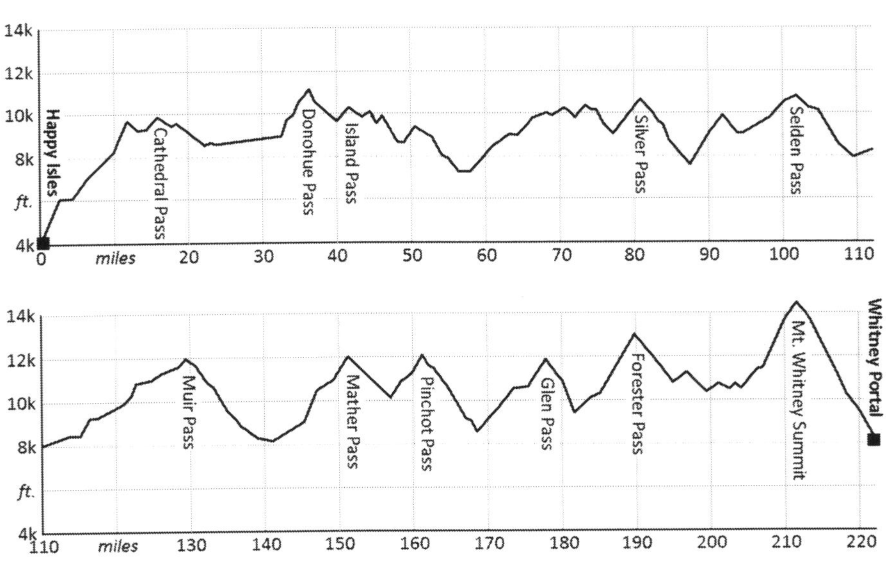

Figure 4 – Elevation Profile and Mountain Passes

Although the treeline is reached at relatively high elevations in the Sierra Nevada (~12,000 ft./3,650m), large stretches of your high alpine journey will take you through sparsely or even entirely unforested areas. There, the open trails provide unobstructed, panoramic views of the surroundings, but, at the same time, it means that shade is a luxury. The later in the summer you hike and the higher up the trail takes you, the more you will be exposed to California's merciless sun. Prepare yourself for a sun intensity you may have never experienced before.

As rivers and creeks are primarily fed by snowmelt, water levels at stream crossings may pose more of a challenge earlier in the hiking season, depending on the amount of snow received during the previous winter months. Most rivers, however, can be crossed by using stepping stones, logs, or footbridges. When crossing on slippery rocks or in places where fording is inevitable, trekking poles or a sturdy stick come in handy to maintain stability. As the season progresses, more and more streams will start to dry up, making crossing much easier.

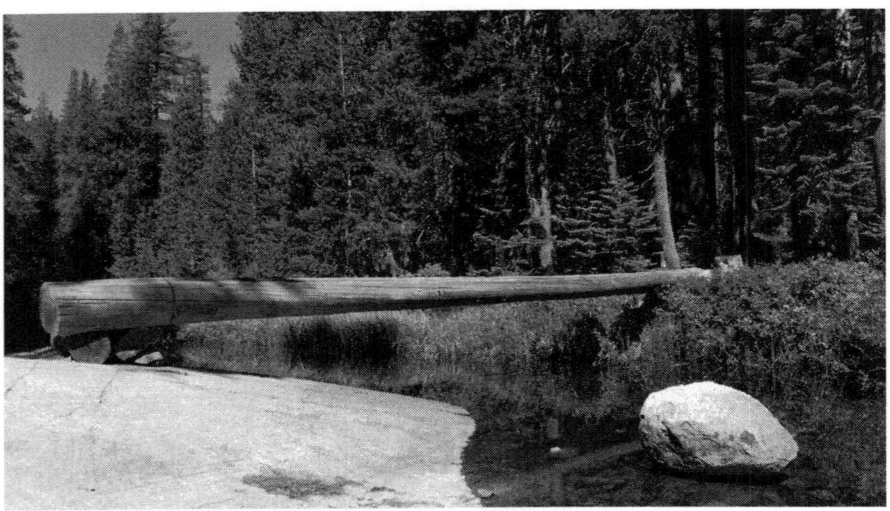

Figure 5 – Log Bridge near Devils Postpile

Trail Access/Exit Points

Figure 6 in combination with Table 1 below provide an overview of popular trailheads along the JMT. There are many other access points, but the ones included here are commonly recognized as some of the more convenient options. All of them can be accessed by car (long-term parking available in most cases). They offer (reasonably) short access to the JMT and are located in close proximity to major travel connections. The trailheads listed herein serve equally well as exit points. Knowing your exit routes is vital in case of emergency, no matter how long of a journey you are planning.

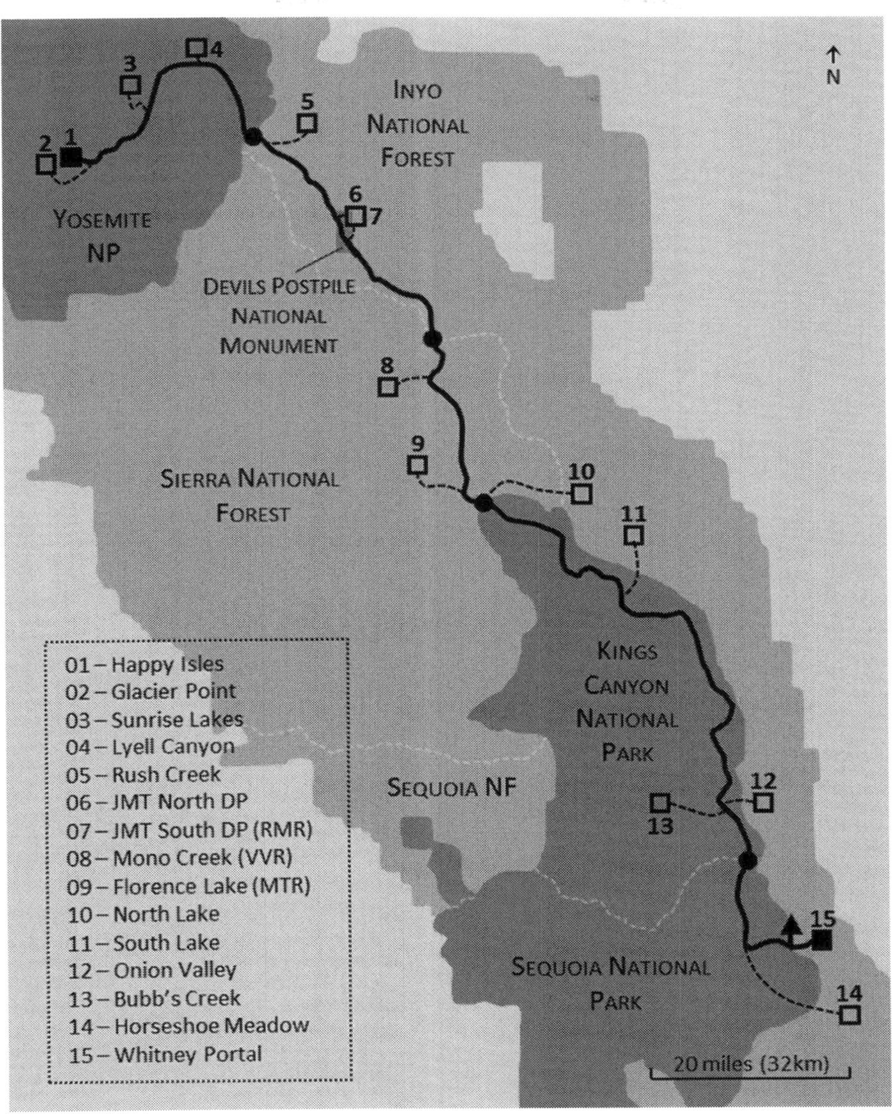

Figure 6 – Overview Map of Trail Access & Exit Points

#	Trailhead (TH)	Dist. to JMT (mi)	Connecting Trail	Access to JMT (mi)	Closest JMT Landmark	Camp at TH	Park at TH*	Closest Travel Connection
1	Happy Isles (YV)	0	n/a	0	Happy Isles Bridge	Yes	Yes	Yosemite V.
2	Glacier Point (YV)	5.6	Panorama	3.3	Nevada Fall	No	No	Yosemite V.
3	Sunrise Lakes (TM)	4.8	Sunrise Lakes	13.4	Sunrise Camp	No	Yes	Lee Vining
4	Lyell Canyon (TM)	0.8	Spur Trail	23.8	Lyell Canyon	Yes	Yes	Lee Vining
5	Rush Creek (Silver Lake)	8.6	Rush Creek	39.7	Thousand Isl. Lake	Yes	Yes	Mammoth
6	Devils Postpile Ranger	0.2	JMT North DP	56.6	Devils Postpile (N)	Yes	Yes	Mammoth
7	Reds Mdw./Rainbow Falls	0.1	JMT South DP	57.3	Devils Postpile (S)	Yes	Yes	Mammoth
8	Mono Creek (Vermillion)	6.1	Lake Edison	87.8	Quail Meadows	Yes	Yes	Fresno
9	Florence Lake	9.1	Florence Lake	107.6	Shooting Star Mdw.	Yes	Yes	Fresno
10	North Lake	15.1	Piute Pass	111.3	Piute Creek	Yes	Yes	Bishop
11	South Lake	11.9	Bishop Pass	136.6	Le Conte Canyon	No	Yes	Bishop
12	Onion Valley	7.0	Kearsarge Pass	179.2	Rae Lakes	Yes	Yes	Bishop
13	Bubbs Creek (Roads End)	12.2	Bubbs Creek	181.3	Rae Lakes	No	Yes	Fresno
14	Horseshoe Meadow	20.4	Cottonwd. Pass	202.3	Crabtree Meadows	Yes	Yes	Lone Pine
15	Whitney Portal	8.8**	Mt. Whitney	208.5	Mt. Whitney	Yes	Yes	Lone Pine

* Always confirm long-term parking availability with local park & forest agencies. Seasonal closures and restrictions may apply.

** Distance from Whitney Portal trailhead to Trail Junction, from where it is an additional 1.9 miles to the summit of Mt. Whitney.

Table 1 – Trail Access & Exit Points (north-to-south)

Trail Sections

If, for whatever reason, you would prefer to walk only a section of the JMT rather than the entire distance, the above table and overview map are a good starting point to tailor your own itinerary. For example, if you would like to complete the JMT in two segments or simply cannot get a permit for starting at the northern or southern end, consider starting your trip in the middle (e.g., TH #9 or #10 in above table). Should you be more interested in weeklong trips, the below list contains popular sections that can be completed in seven days or less (based on a 12-mile average per day):

- Devils Postpile to Happy Isles (~55 miles)
- Devils Postpile to North Lake (~66 miles)
- North Lake to South Lake "Loop" (~53 miles)
- South Lake to Onion Valley (~60 miles)
- Onion Valley to Whitney Portal (~47 miles; incl. Mt. Whitney)
- Onion Valley to Horseshoe Meadow (~64 miles; incl. Whitney)

All of these multi-day section hikes are described in more detail in Appendix D. The descriptions include exact distances, elevation changes, trip durations, difficulty levels, highlights, and elevation profiles.

Navigation & Maps

Following a clearly visible path, it is generally easy to navigate along the JMT, although trail markers and sign posts are somewhat scarce. They are predominantly found in the more popular parts of the trail, like Yosemite Valley and Mt. Whitney, which is also where you are most likely to encounter larger crowds. Over the entire length of the trail, there is a respectable number of side trails diverting from the main route, so you are well-advised to carry a map or navigational aid of some sort in order to stay on the right path. Whenever you enter an area with several side trails providing access to the JMT, you will notice an uptick in traffic typically caused by day hikers.

Figure 7 – Trail Signs along JMT

Below is a (non-exhaustive) overview of available printed and electronic maps that are widely recommended for the JMT. Although not necessarily required, it is advisable to carry a compass and know how to use it in case of emergency.

Printed Maps

- Tom Harrison's JMT Map-Pack: Topographic map printed on 13 waterproof, tear-resistant plastic pages (8.5"x11"), scaled at 1:63,360. The map is durable, small, and covers the entire trail.
- Erik the Black's JMT Pocket Atlas: Pocket-sized full-color booklet (5"x8") that includes topographic maps of the entire trail, data tables, elevation profiles, GPS waypoints, campsites, etc.

Electronic Maps

- Guthook's JMT Guide ($): JMT-specific app that uses phone's GPS to pinpoint location on the trail. Downloadable map includes water sources, tent sites, points of interest, and other features. Elevation profile shows current location and upcoming terrain.
- Gaia GPS ($): Versatile hiking and outdoor app that offers terrain, topo, and aerial maps for download. Uses phone's GPS to show location on the trail. App lets you plan trips, record tracks, create waypoints, and take geo-tagged photos.

- CalTopo, SierraMapper, AllTrails (free/$): Online mapping tools that allow you to plot your own routes, save and print topographic maps, and download waypoints to GPS devices.

Trail Use Regulations

Over the course of your 221-mile journey, you will pass through a number of wilderness areas that are managed by different national park and national forest authorities (see Figure 6 on page 13). It is worth noting that national parks and national forests serve very distinct purposes and allow different ranges of use. National parks emphasize strict preservation of pristine areas and focus on protecting natural and historic resources. National forests emphasize resource preservation but also allow other kinds of use, including lumber, cattle grazing, hunting, and recreation with or without vehicles. Because of these differences, adjoining national parks and national forests may have different rules for entering and using their designated wilderness areas. Table 2 below summarizes the most relevant commonalities and differences in terms of applicable rules. Regulations marked with an asterisk (*) are further specified in subsequent sections of this book.

<table>
<tr><th>Regulation</th><th>National Parks</th><th>National Forests</th></tr>
<tr><td>Permit*</td><td colspan="2">A valid wilderness permit is required for all overnight wilderness use.</td></tr>
<tr><td>Wild Camping*</td><td colspan="2">Wild camping is generally allowed; area-specific restrictions apply.</td></tr>
<tr><td>Food Storage*</td><td colspan="2">Use of approved bear-resistant containers is mandatory. Pack out all trash.</td></tr>
<tr><td>Wood Fires*</td><td colspan="2">Wood fires are allowed in existing fire rings; area-specific restrictions apply.</td></tr>
<tr><td>Fishing</td><td colspan="2">Fishing is permitted with valid California fishing license. All pertinent CA fishing regulations apply.</td></tr>
<tr><td>Vehicles</td><td colspan="2">Motorized or mechanical equipment (incl. bicycles) is prohibited in wilderness areas.</td></tr>
</table>

Pets/Stock	All pets are prohibited. Stock use is limited to 25 head.	Domestic pets are allowed. Stock use is limited to 25 head.
Bear Spray	Possession and use prohibited.	Carrying EPA-registered bear spray is allowed.
Weapons	Concealed carry (CCW) is allowed with valid CA permit. Discharging weapons for any reason is illegal.	CCW is allowed with valid CA permit. Discharging weapons is prohibited, except for emergencies and taking of game as permitted by CA state law.
Drones/UAS	Unmanned aircraft systems (UAS) are prohibited, incl. drones and other remotely piloted vehicles.	UAS cannot take off from, land in, or be operated from designated wilderness areas.

Table 2 – Trail Use Regulations

! If you intend to walk the JMT in its entirety, you are well-advised to plan your gear and itinerary in accordance with the more restrictive national park rules and be sure to fully understand all applicable wilderness regulations and area-specific restrictions before you set out.

b. Points of Interest

The JMT is studded with scenic attractions that will vie for your attention and provide many pleasant distractions along the way. Be sure to budget time to fully enjoy these points of interest that add to the overall experience and make this a truly memorable journey. Starting at Yosemite Valley and travelling southbound, this section presents some of the highlights that you will not want to miss.

Yosemite Valley: Marking the northern terminus of the JMT, Yosemite Valley is the heart of the surrounding Yosemite National Park. Each year, the park welcomes over four million visitors from all over the globe, who are eager to explore the glacial valley and the towering granite peaks that surround it. Outstanding natural beauty and world-famous landmarks, such as Half Dome, El Capitan, and Yosemite Falls (highest in North America), create the perfect setting for starting an epic adventure on the John Muir Trail – which, by itself, represents a major attraction in Yosemite.

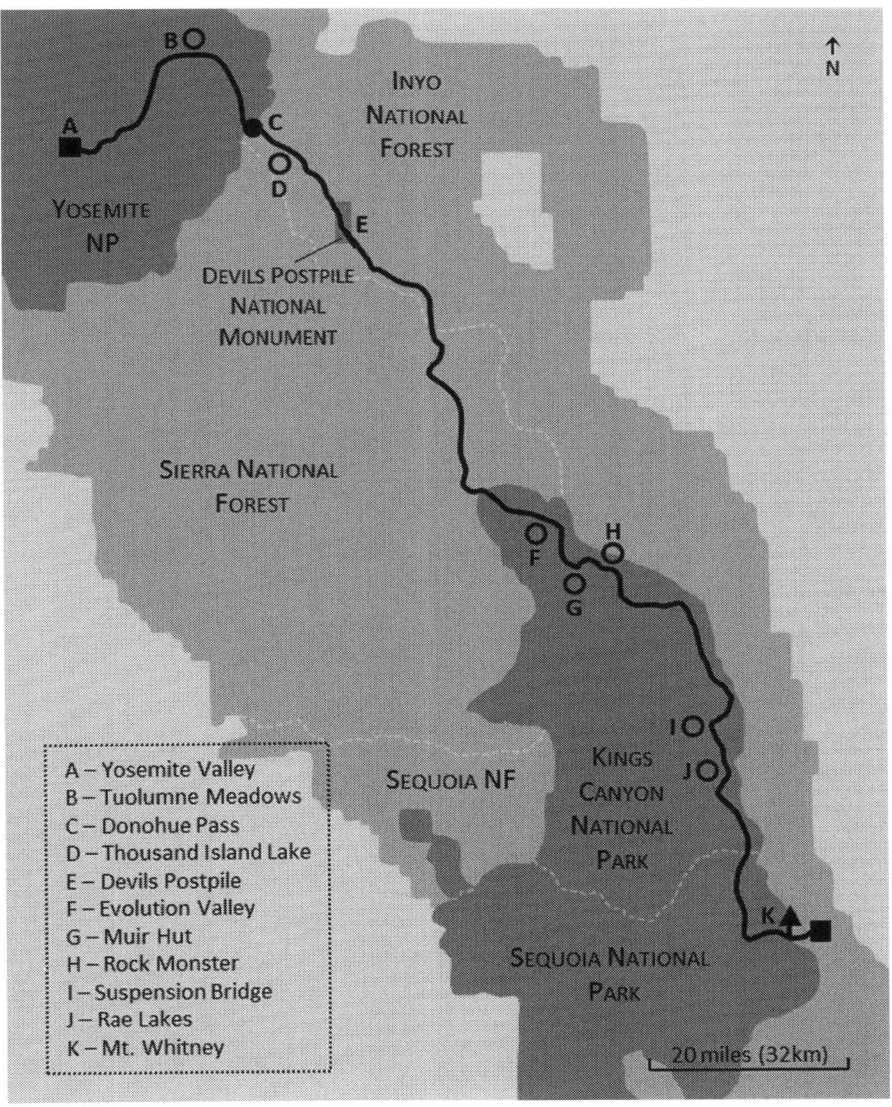

Figure 8 – Overview Map of Points of Interest

Tuolumne Meadows: Surrounded by rugged mountain peaks and glacially-carved domes, Tuolumne Meadows is one of the largest high-elevation meadows in the Sierra Nevada. Its subalpine landscape is dominated by the Tuolumne River which cascades peacefully along a meandering channel. The meadow's vegetation is also supported by a system of snowmelt-fed creeks which cause large areas of the meadow to flood periodically, especially in springtime. Interestingly, most of the water that filters through Tuolumne Meadows becomes drinking water for San Francisco, requiring only minimal treatment due to its high level of purity.

Donohue Pass: Marking the boundary between Yosemite National Park and Inyo National Forest (Ansel Adams Wilderness), Donohue Pass is located between Mount Lyell and Donohue Peak, approximately 1 mile past the last Lyell Fork crossing. At 11,066 ft. (3,373m), it is the sixth highest of the ten named mountain passes on the John Muir Trail. In 2015, Donohue Pass gained mainstream fame due to the introduction of an interim quota to limit the number of hikers exiting the Yosemite Wilderness over the pass.

Thousand Island Lake: In a picture-perfect setting, Thousand Island Lake is located at the base of Banner Peak (12,942 ft./ 3,945m), the second tallest peak in the Sierra Nevada's Ritter Range. The lake itself is a large tarn formed in the bottom of a cirque that has been excavated by a glacier. Characteristic for the lake are the many small rocky islands that stud its surface. Thousand Island Lake is the source of the Middle Fork of the San Joaquin River, which runs down into the San Joaquin Valley.

Devils Postpile National Monument: The national monument protects and preserves two main attractions: the basalt columns of Devils Postpile and the 101-foot-high Rainbow Falls. Created by a lava flow over 80,000 years ago and gradually excavated during several glacial periods, Devils Postpile ranks as one of the world's finest examples of columnar basalt, displaying an unusual symmetry. Its beautifully straight columns tower up to 60 feet (18m) high and average 2 feet (60cm) in diameter. Their predominant shape is hexagonal, but some of the columns have different polygonal cross-sections. The differences in shape are best seen at the top of the rock formation, which is accessible to visitors.

Evolution Valley & Lake: From the San Joaquin River to Muir Pass, the JMT traverses the Evolution Region, an area that owes its designation to a group of mountains named for important scientists associated with the theory of evolution (e.g., Mount Darwin, Mount Mendel, Mount Spencer, and Mount Huxley). The trail follows Evolution Creek through Evolution Valley, which is filled with gentle meadows and graceful lodgepole pines. McClure Meadow is a particularly popular spot for its excellent views of The Hermit, another prominent peak in the area. On your ascent to Evolution Basin, you will pass Evolution Lake, peacefully mirroring its high alpine surroundings.

Muir Hut: Suitably located at the top of Muir Pass, the iconic stone hut was constructed to preserve the memory of John Muir and to serve as a temporary shelter for hikers caught in adverse conditions on this exposed section of the trail. Erected in 1930 by the Sierra Club in cooperation with the Sierra National Forest, the marvelous structure is built entirely of stone collected from the area. Fuel and all other building materials, including sand for mortar, had to be packed to the site on mules. A plaque above the decommissioned fireplace inside the shelter briefly summarizes the hut's history and reminds visitors that overnight camping and fires are prohibited.

! Without a doubt, the Muir Hut is an outstanding landmark and photo opportunity. First and foremost, however, it is a monument and deserves to be treated as such. Never climb on top of the shelter and refrain from camping in it unless it is an emergency!

Rock Monster: Lurking somewhere between Starr Camp and Big Pete's Meadow, the gluttonous Rock Monster (a.k.a. Whale Rock) awaits unsuspecting hikers passing through Le Conte Canyon. The peculiar-looking rock formation resembles a wide open mouth with smaller rocks neatly arranged inside of it to serve as teeth. Admittedly ranking lower on the historic/scenic significance scale, the Rock Monster offers a bit of amusement and makes for a cheerful picture to show folks at home.

Woods Creek Suspension Bridge: Another impressive man-made structure on the trail is the suspension bridge over Woods Creek, just a short distance from the Woods Creek Trail junction. Spanning roughly 90 feet (27m) across the rushing creek, the bridge not only stands out for its elegant construction but also for the fact that no effort was spared to build something this intricate so far from civilization. Signs on either end of the bridge advise hikers to cross one at a time. You will know why once you get there.

Rae Lakes: A series of three sapphire blue lakes sitting in a high country basin against a backdrop of rugged granite peaks. The area is renowned for its exceptional beauty and stunning views of the towering Painted Lady and Fin Dome. JMT/PCT hikers are likely to encounter other backpackers on their journey to complete the 40-mile Rae Lakes Loop, one of the most popular multi-day hikes in Sequoia and Kings Canyon National Parks.

Mt. Whitney: With a summit elevation of 14,505 ft. (4,421m) above sea level, Mt. Whitney is the highest peak in the contiguous United States – a trophy that hikers from all over the world are eager to bag each year. From the top, you are treated to an incredible 360-degree panoramic view of the Sierra Nevada. While there, take a moment to explore the Smithsonian Institution Shelter, a stone hut built in the early 1900s to house scientific studies of high altitude phenomena as well as spectroscopic observations of Mars.

c. Weather

The best time to hike the JMT is between June and September. During these months, you will have a very low chance of encountering any significant snow in most parts. The weather will generally be warmer and the days will be longer, giving you more time to hike and reducing the amount of gear you have to carry for cold and/or snowy conditions.

Temperature

The most important measure in deciding what kind of gear and clothing to bring is the expected temperature. Table 3 below shows average annual temperatures at Yosemite Park Headquarters (4,000 ft./1,220m). In order to estimate the temperatures along the trail, it is helpful to use a lapse rate. As a rule of thumb, deduct 5°F for every 1,000 ft. in elevation gain (3°C for every 300m) from the respective temperature of your hiking month.

Month	°F (low/high)	°C (low/high)
January	29 / 48	-2 / 9
February	30 / 51	-1 / 11
March	34 / 58	1 / 14
April	38 / 64	3 / 18
May	45 / 71	7 / 22
June	51 / 81	11 / 27
July	57 / 89	14 / 32
August	56 / 89	13 / 32
September	51 / 82	11 / 28
October	42 / 71	6 / 22
November	33 / 56	1 / 13
December	28 / 47	-2 / 8

Source: U.S. Climate Data; Period 1981-2010.

Table 3 – Average Temperatures at Yosemite Park Headquarters

For example, if you plan to start in Yosemite Valley (4,000 ft.) in July, you can expect temperatures of 57-89°F. As you reach Tuolumne Meadows (~9,000 ft.) a few days later, temperatures will have likely dropped by ~25°F [= ((9,000 ft. - 4,000 ft.) / 1,000 ft.) * 5°F] to 32-64°F. After further hiking over passes above 12,000 feet, your maximum temperature may only be around 50°F. However, you will rarely find yourself camping above 10,000 feet where temperatures typically range from 27-59°F.

If you are hiking between June and September, prepare for spending the majority of your days in temperatures of 50-70°F (10-20°C) during the day and 25-50°F (-4-10°C) at night. As you ascend to higher elevations, you are likely to pass patches of snow in August still. The changes in temperature in the High Sierra can be considerable and require both light and airy day clothes as well as insulated warm evening clothing. Although hard to imagine, one day you might be drenched in sweat climbing out of Yosemite Valley or Whitney Portal at 90°F (30°C) and then, only two days later, your sleeping bag can be frozen solid to your tent.

It is also important to keep in mind that you will be hiking at elevations well above 9,000 feet for a great portion of the trail. This means that, while temperatures may be fairly low during the day, the sun will be radiating mercilessly. Once this source of warmth sets behind other peaks, however, temperatures will drop quickly. Additionally, any water you will find for washing clothes and yourself will likely be around 40-60°F (4-15°C). Keep this in mind when planning your arrivals to camp. At the end of a long day, your energy and body heat fade rapidly. While you will want to wash off dust and sweat, regaining a comfortable temperature becomes a challenge after sunset.

ⓘ Setting out early in the morning will allow you to cover more distance before the sun gets too hot and to arrive at camp and get washed up while the sun is still out and strong enough to dry/warm you.

Precipitation

If you are hiking between late June and September, it will only rain occasionally, if at all. The amount of rain can vary from a brief downpour to a light drizzle over hours. Afternoon thunderstorms are not uncommon in the region but should pass fairly quickly. As clouds start to form, it is good to get your light rain jacket readily available at the top of your pack. It is unlikely that you will encounter any snow during this time of year, except maybe for scattered patches at higher elevations.

Table 4 below shows the average annual precipitation and snowfall at the Yosemite Park Headquarters (4,000 ft./1,220m).

Month	Precipitation		Snowfall	
	(inch)	(mm)	(inch)	(cm)
Jan	6.5	165.1	17	43.2
Feb	6.7	170.2	4	10.2
Mar	5.2	132.1	5	12.7
Apr	2.8	71.1	1	2.5
May	1.7	43.2	0	0.0
Jun	0.7	17.8	0	0.0
Jul	0.4	10.2	0	0.0
Aug	0.1	2.5	0	0.0
Sep	0.7	17.8	0	0.0
Oct	2.1	53.3	0	0.0
Nov	4.6	116.8	3	7.6
Dec	5.4	137.2	5	12.7

Source: U.S. Climate Data; Period 1981-2010.

Table 4 – Average Precipitation and Snowfall at Yosemite Park Headquarters

As for weather patterns, "it never rains at night in the Sierra" seems to hold true for the most part. After long stretches of clear skies, clouds may appear and often build up during the day while vanishing at night. With every additional day on the trail, your chances of getting rained on at some point increase. At the same time, heavy rain or even hail at night are possible, especially when a late summer/fall storm rolls in. Be aware of your camp surrounding when this happens and prepare to seek shelter away from any metal objects, including your tent.

! Remember, when seeking shelter during a thunderstorm, move away from freestanding trees and place your pack and other metal objects at a distance. Avoid passes and peaks (especially Mt. Whitney) and stay low to the ground among scattered boulders or trees.

For comparison, the temperature and precipitation data for the Mt. Whitney end of the JMT is very similar:

"Ninety five percent of total precipitation (which includes both rain and snow) falls between the months of October and May, with more than half falling in January, February, and March. The frequency of summer showers increase at higher elevations and, correspondingly, there are more cloudy days. But even though these thundershowers are of short duration, they are still a danger to the hiker/climber on the summit or high ridges on Mt. Whitney and other Sierra Peaks. That being said, if you detect a thunderstorm developing, vacate the summit and high ridges at once. The first recorded fatality on Mt Whitney was due to lightning."[1]

Looking at both temperature and precipitation, it becomes clear why June, July, August, and September are the most desirable but also the busiest months to hike the JMT.

d. Camping

Overnight camping is generally allowed on the JMT, except where prohibited. There is plenty of opportunity to set up camp along the route, and sleeping amidst breathtakingly beautiful mountain scenery far away from all the real world hustle and bustle is one of the many highlights the 221-mile journey has to offer.

---

[1] Source: *http://timberlinetrails.net/WhitneyWeather.html*

Regulations

In addition to the rules for what you can take with you on the JMT and how you should use the trail, there are also rules for setting up and using campsites. These rules help minimize the impact that visitors have, keep the wilderness wild, and ensure that all hikers can enjoy their time on the JMT.

General Camping Rules:

Wilderness regulations and common sense command hikers to only use previously impacted campsites. These campsites are neither marked nor equipped with picnic benches. They are simply flattened or cleared patches that have been established in accordance with generally accepted camping guidelines (i.e., not on vegetation and at least 100 feet (30m) away from any water source or trail). If you come across an established campsite that does not meet the required distances, refrain from using it, unless your only other option would be to impact live vegetation. There is no shortage of properly established campsites along the JMT, giving you a wide variety of spots to choose from.

[!] In order to restore overused areas, wilderness officials have started to remove previously impacted campsites that do not meet the above-stated distance requirements. Hikers are requested to support this effort by camping only in adequately established sites.

Area-Specific Camping Restrictions:

- No camping within four trail miles of Tuolumne Meadows, Yosemite Valley, Glacier Point and one air mile from any road in Yosemite NP.
- No camping at Shadow Lake or within a quarter mile of the outflow of Garnet Lake or Thousand Island Lake.
- No camping outside of established campgrounds at Devils Postpile National Monument.
- No camping at Timberline Lake (located before Guitar Lake).

- Two-night camping limit in Crabtree/Whitney Creek area and at Guitar Lake.
- Three-night camping limit at Lower and Upper Soldier Lakes.

Food Storage:

- All food and scented items must be stored in an approved bear-resistant container.
- Along most stretches of the JMT, especially at Yosemite and Mt. Whitney, it is mandated to carry a portable bear canister.
- Permanent bear boxes are available at sporadic locations, but they *do not* represent a viable alternative for JMT thru-hikers.

! Keeping human food away from animals, in particular bears, is of utmost importance not only for your own safety but also for the well-being of the animals. In line with the (un)popular saying "A fed bear is a dead bear"[2], several bears have to be killed each year for safety reasons as a result of the irreversible actions of careless humans.

Human Waste:

- Human waste must be buried at least 6 inches (15cm) deep and 200 feet (60m) from trails, campsites, and water sources.
- All toilet paper should be packed out rather than buried in the ground as it is often dug up and spread by animals in search of food. A simple zip lock bag generally suffices for this purpose.
- Inside the Whitney Zone (essentially covering Trail Crest to Whitney Portal) you are not allowed to bury human waste. It, along with any toilet paper, must be packed out in a waste bag (which you will receive when you pick up your permit).

Campfires

Along the JMT, wood campfires are subject to restrictions and other requirements that hikers need to be aware of and abide by at all times. As

---

[2] Source: *https://www.nps.gov/depo/planyourvisit/keeping-wildlife-wild.htm*

a general rule, you are only allowed to start a campfire in pre-existing fire rings. Since dead wood is an important fertilizer, campfires are prohibited in certain areas where such biofuels are extremely scarce due to limited vegetation. See Table 5 below for area-specific restrictions.

Area	Restriction
Yosemite NP	- No campfires above 9,000 ft. - Additional seasonal restrictions may apply
Inyo NF	- No campfires above 10,000 ft. - No campfires at some locations below 10,000 ft. from Donohue Pass to Shadow Creek - No campfires at Duck Creek or Purple Lake
Devils Postpile NM	- No campfires outside of designated fire rings
Sierra NF	- No campfires above 10,000 ft. north of the San Joaquin River/Kings River Divide - No campfires above 10,400 ft. south of the San Joaquin River/Kings River Divide.
SEKI NP	- No campfires above 10,000 ft. - No campfires in Granite Basin and Redwood Canyon

Table 5 – Area-Specific Campfire Restrictions

There may be additional site-specific restrictions, and campfires may be banned entirely in times of drought. That said, refraining from campfires altogether, thereby decreasing the risk of wildfires and conserving limited biofuels, has a strong advocacy.

! Exercise extreme caution anytime you decide to start a campfire. Keep the fire small and use sticks no bigger than the size of one or two of your fingers together. Lighting a campfire in the wilderness is a great responsibility and can turn into a major disaster if not properly handled.

Another permit you will need within the National Forest sections of the JMT is a California Campfire Permit. Even if you don't plan on having a campfire, it is still required for operating a camp stove in the wilderness. The permit is free and can be obtained at any CA Forest Service ranger station or online at *http://www.preventwildfireca.org/*.

Choosing a Wild Camping Site

Established campsites are plentiful along the JMT. However, if you find yourself camping in between sites or if you plan on taking side trips off the trail, consider the following factors when choosing a campsite:

Comfort – Avoid camping in basins and dips, where cold air will gather, and in close proximity to water. Moisture and dew can attract mosquitos, soak your gear, or cover it in frost. Moving just a few steps up and away from these areas can make for a much more comfortable night. At the same time, you want to have reasonably easy access to water for washing and cooking. Ideally, your campsite will also provide wind shelter while allowing the sun to shine brightly from the east to warm and dry your tent and sleeping bag in the morning. Choose dry sand or small gravel over any organic substance and vegetation to prevent moisture from creeping into your tent through the floor.

Strategy – Pick campsites that are convenient milestones for the distance and difficulty of each trail section. You will find that the existing campsites are often ideally located in this regard. Many are located just before particularly difficult sections of the trail, enabling you to tackle the most challenging portion of your day early on, when your legs are fresh and temperatures not too hot.

Impact on Nature – Minimizing your environmental impact helps preserve the trail and surrounding areas for fellow hikers and future generations. Here are a few basic principles you should follow when choosing a campsite (as recommended by the Leave No Trace Center for Outdoor Ethics):

- Camp on durable surfaces such as rock, gravel, sand, or snow; avoid any type of vegetation if possible
- Camp at previously impacted sites or places that are suitable for camping as-is, i.e., you do not have to move rocks, branches, etc.
- Keep your campsite as small as possible
- Camp at least 200 feet (60m) from lakes and streams

Safety – Do not camp under or near dead trees! Falling trees or limbs pose a severe safety hazard and should not be underestimated, especially during windy conditions. Therefore, be sure to always check overhead first before choosing a campsite in the woods.

Established Campgrounds

Although the majority of the trip will require camping in nature, relying solely on the comforts you decided to carry along, there a few locations along the trail, where hikers could enjoy a few real-world luxuries if desired. The available amenities range from simple vault toilets to complete bathrooms with showers. Some of these locations can be reserved in advance, whereas others are only available on a first-come, first-served basis. The campsite listing provided in Appendix C also includes available campground options (incl. amenities). During peak season, many of these campgrounds are high in demand and can get very crowded. Tuolumne Meadows and Red's Meadow, for instance, are known to get extremely busy during the height of the summer.

ⓘ If you intend to spend the night at one of the first-come, first-served sites, you are well-advised to arrive earlier in the day to secure a spot, as these can fill up quickly.

e. Water

There is plenty. Even in late August, after three months of hardly any rain, the abundant snowfalls of winter and spring still feed the countless rivers and lakes. Large parts of the JMT will take you right along beautiful bodies of water – babbling in brooks or resting peacefully in tarns, reflecting the surrounding peaks. You will rarely walk for more than an hour before a stream crosses your path, so water availability should not be an issue. That said, it is still wise to plan out your water resupply points to make sure you are carrying enough to drink throughout the day, but not so much that it adds unnecessary weight to your pack. Larger streams and lakes are more likely to have water in them than smaller ponds and creeks which may be seasonal. With regards to quality, it is best to get your water from sources that are moving and deep rather than shallow and stagnant.

ⓘ All National Park Services recommend treating any water you consume. Even if you decide to ignore this advice, you can minimize the risk by opting for water sources that are less accessible to wildlife or other humans. Moving 50 feet (15m) or so upstream from any trail crossing or using water that is flowing down steep slopes will further reduce the likelihood of contamination.

Furthermore, be aware that while the water looks clear, it may be contaminated. The global prevalence of the protozoan Giardia lamblia and the E.coli bacteria does not stop in the Sierra Nevada. Both lead to diarrhea and abdominal cramps, sometimes with a delay of 5-15 days post exposure. Fortunately, both can be filtered and/or killed with common treatment methods (more on that in Section 6d *Food & Water*). Maintaining a good camp hygiene is equally important to limit the spread of microbe-borne illness, especially after a squat with a view. When choosing your loo, keep a distance of at least 200 feet (60m) to any campsites, trails, and sources of water. This is the best precaution to avoid further contamination. The same applies to washing yourself, your clothing, or cooking utensils. Opt for biodegradable soap or, ideally, refrain from using any kind of detergent altogether.

f. Flora & Fauna

The Sierra Nevada is not only famed for its striking geology but also for the wide variety of plants and animals which inhabit the region. Different ecological communities are found along the gradually changing elevations of the mountain range. These so-called 'biotic zones' (or 'life zones') can be broadly divided into Foothills (below 3,500 ft.), Montane (3,500 ft. - 9,000 ft.), and Alpine (above 9,000 ft.). Each of these zones supports a different ecosystem with its own distinct vegetation and wildlife. The JMT passes only through the Montane and Alpine zones.

Vegetation

The following are some of the most common plants that you are likely to see along the JMT:

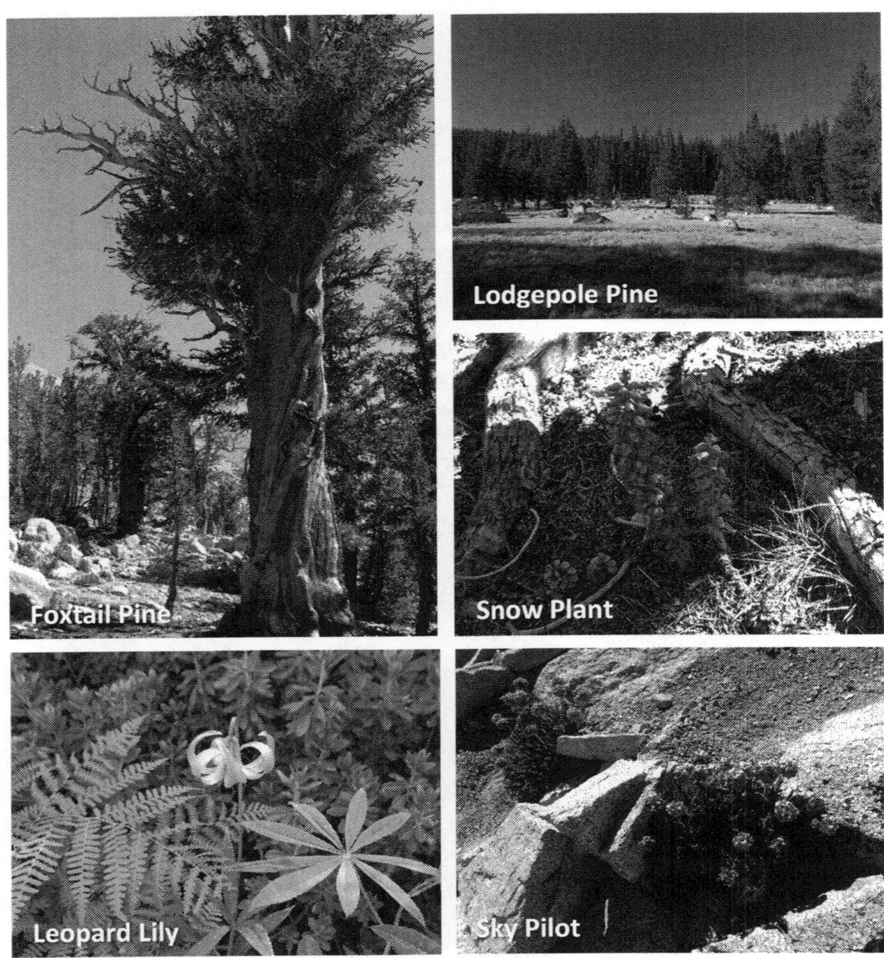

At lower elevations, you will also walk beneath white fir, sugar pine, and incense cedar. Large areas of the montane forest are populated with Jeffrey pine, a tall evergreen conifer that is easily identified by its distinct resin scent, commonly said to resemble vanilla or butterscotch. Higher up, you will wander amidst mountain hemlock and whitebark pine and feast your eyes on extensive subalpine meadows showcasing wildflowers galore.

Wildlife

Below are some of the more prominent animals that you are likely to encounter during your journey on the JMT:

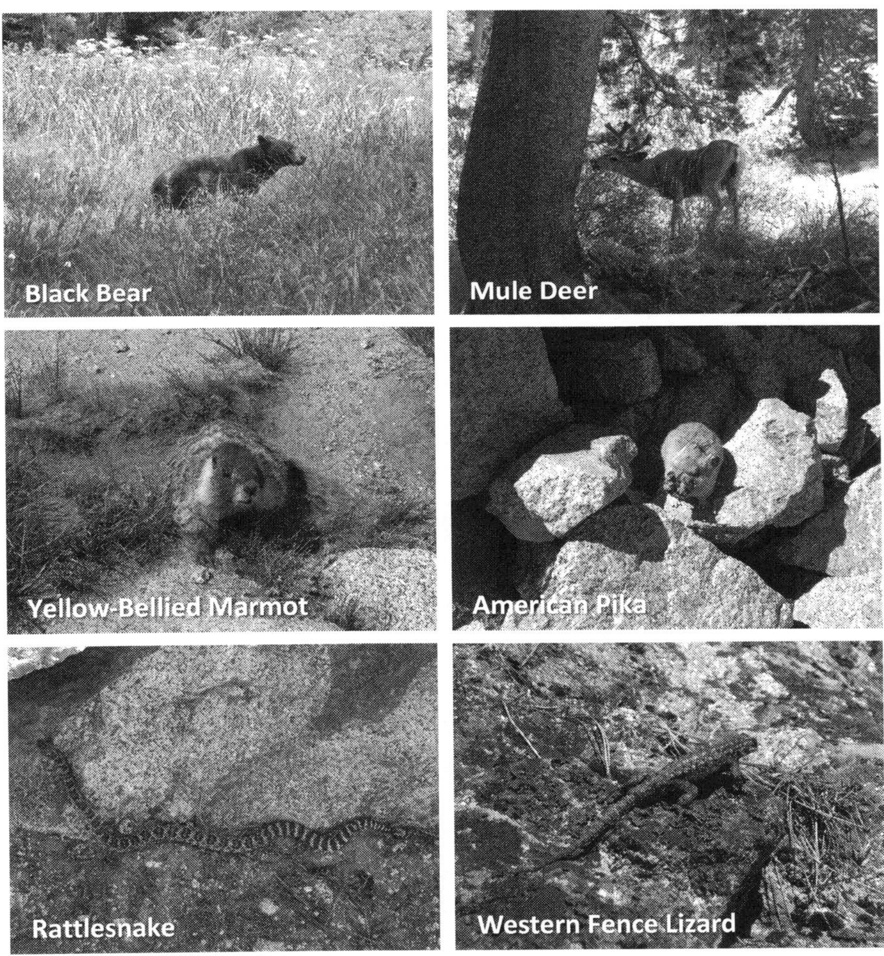

Additionally, observant hikers will notice ashy-grey Clark's nutcrackers swooping among subalpine forests, flashing their black-and-white wings and tail feathers. At higher elevations, the squeaking calls of chipmunks and ground squirrels will announce their presence long before you're able to spot the nimble rodents. Although extremely rare, you may even catch sight of a mountain lion or the Sierra Nevada's endangered bighorn sheep.

! Please respect animals by giving them a wide berth. Never feed or approach them. Keep your distance even if they approach you.

In summary, the JMT will bring you face to face with some truly stunning features of the natural world. This short section doesn't begin to do justice to all that you will see on the trail. If you are interested in learning more, there are a number of books and online resources that provide far more information than this guide will be able to cover. Recommendations for additional reading are provided in Appendix I *Links & References*.

g. Safety

Safety is an important part of any trip, but even more so when you are hiking through remote wilderness where it will be difficult to get help during an emergency. Safety on the JMT means, among other things, that you are well prepared for the hike, have the right gear, are in good physical shape, understand how to avoid dangerous situations, and are prepared to deal with emergencies if they arise. Different people may define safety differently, but everyone should understand the risks of a long hike through the mountains before deciding to hit the trail.[3]

Travel

Being located in the United States, traveling to and from the JMT is probably not as significant a safety concern as it could be in other parts of the world. Even so, you should still exercise caution in getting to and from the trailheads and understand the risks of what you are doing. This is particularly true if you decide to hitchhike. It is relatively common for hikers to hitchhike from Whitney Portal down to the town of Lone Pine in order to link up with other transportation options. Whether you decide to hitchhike and for what portions of your trip is ultimately up to you and at your own risk.

---

[3] The safety notes described in this section as well as the comments on other conditions in the following section are extracted in large part from the guidebook *Plan & Go | High Sierra Trail* (Sandiburg Press 2016).

! If you decide to travel by car, be aware that bears are not uncommon at either trailhead. Do not leave any food in your car and do not leave any coolers visible. Bears know what coolers look like and are more than willing to do some work to find out what's inside yours.

Camping

Before you pitch your tent at night, it's a good idea to take a look at your surroundings to make sure you're not pitching it on top of an anthill or next to a dead tree that could potentially fall over. Animals, such as rodents and bears, shouldn't be too interested in you unless you have food in your tent or you smell like food. Best practices are to never take anything scented into the tent with you at night. This means no food, no drinks other than water, no delicious-tasting lip balms, etc. If you cooked anything particularly pungent or spilled food on your clothes, you might also want to consider leaving them outside your tent in the vestibule or elsewhere. Make sure all your food is in your bear canister and both your canister and clothes are secured to something so animals can't run off with them. Pile rocks on top of them, wedge them into trees, etc.

Bears

Although relatively rare, it is not uncommon to see bears in this part of the Sierra Nevada. Black bears are the only species of bears found in the wild in California. Despite their name, the color can range from black to a cinnamon brown, the latter being more common in California. Here are a few ways to reduce your chances of running into a bear on the JMT:

- Make noise when you're walking. Talking, singing, banging your hiking poles together every so often, etc. are great ways to give the rest of nature some advanced notice of your presence.
- Don't keep any food or other scented items inside your tent and put bear canisters at least 30 feet (9m) from your tent at night.
- Use the permanent bear boxes in addition to the canisters when they are available. If you're not familiar, bear boxes are large steel containers with locking doors that bears can't open.

! Refer to the National Park Service website for additional advice on how to deal with black bear encounters and remember that bear spray is not allowed on the JMT.

Snakes

Rattlesnakes inhabit many regions of California and can live at elevations up to around 10,000 ft. (3,048m). While this means that you have the potential to run into rattlesnakes during most of the JMT, you are more likely to find them in the warmer, lower elevation portions of the trail, like Yosemite National Park. The main thing you want to avoid is startling them. This includes stepping on them, stepping near them, or otherwise coming into close proximity. Rattlesnakes can sense you coming through the vibrations in the ground and are likely to get out of the way, provided they have enough time to do so. They don't want to run into you any more than you want to run into them. Here are a few tips to help you avoid a bad encounter with a rattlesnake:

- Only step where you can clearly see the ground. This means that you shouldn't be stepping into bushes or tall grass, over logs or rocks, or otherwise placing your feet anywhere you can't see beforehand.
- Don't stick your hands anywhere you can't see. Fortunately, there are few if any places on the JMT where your hands will need to be involved in moving you, so you won't often find yourself putting your hands in places where a rattlesnake could be sitting.
- If you have to step somewhere you can't see, it's a good idea to walk slowly, stomp your feet, and use your hiking poles to probe at the path in front of you before stepping forward.

! You can find more information about how to avoid and deal with rattlesnakes here: *https://www.wildlife.ca.gov/News/Snake*

Altitude Sickness

You'll have several days where you ascend and descend thousands of feet and reach elevations as high as 14,505 feet (4,421m) at the summit of Mt. Whitney. At these elevations, it is very possible that you could succumb to altitude sickness, which occurs when you cannot get enough oxygen from the "thinner" air at high altitudes. This causes symptoms such as a headache, loss of appetite, and trouble sleeping. It happens most often when people who are not used to oxygen-deficient air go quickly from lower elevations to 8,000 feet (2,438m) or higher. It is recommended that JMT hikers understand the symptoms of altitude sickness and are prepared to deal with them.

ⓘ For more information on the subject and good advice on preventative measures, check out the 'Altitude Acclimatization' group on Facebook or conduct your own research.

River Crossings

During the summer months, rivers and creeks tend to swell due to runoff from snowmelt, resulting in potentially dangerous conditions. Powerful current, icy water, and river obstructions can trap or harm the unwary. Stay away from river and creek banks during high water conditions and avoid rock hopping, as stream-polished rocks may be slippery. If you have to ford a stream, avoid deep and/or swift water. To prevent being pulled under by its weight, unbuckle your pack's waist strap, so you can quickly shed it if you fall in. If crossing on a natural bridge of rocks or logs, consider where you will land if you fall. Never cross above rapids or falls.

(i) If possible, pay attention to stream crossings when planning your itinerary. Trying to cross rivers and creeks earlier in the day is advisable as it will leave enough time for you (and potentially your gear) to dry before getting to camp at night.

General Precautions

Whether you are hiking solo or with a buddy, it is always a good idea to inform a third party about your detailed hiking plans. Be aware that cell phone reception is spotty at best along the JMT. Carrying a simple whistle will increase your chances of getting help sooner in case of emergency. Some hikers may even opt to take along more advanced gadgets like satellite messengers or personal locator beacons (PLB).

h. Other Conditions

Wildfires

Wildfires are an unpredictable but common occurrences in California. In 2013, forest fires devastated large areas in the Yosemite Wilderness and around Mammoth. The fires never got close enough to the JMT to pose an immediate threat to hikers, but the intermittent thick smoke made breathing harder and reduced visibility. As a precaution, be sure to know your exit routes on the trail and call the ranger station or permit office closest to your trailhead to inquire about current conditions before you set out. When on the trail, ask hikers coming your way and stop at the scattered ranger stations to get the latest updates. If you are made aware of any potential and existing fire threats in your area, be sure to adjust your hiking itinerary accordingly. If you experience shortness of breath, chest pain, rapid heart rate, or fatigue, take breaks more frequently or consider exiting the trail altogether and continue your adventure another time.

Rockslides & Flash Floods

You will be hiking in mountainous areas where landslides or rockslides could be triggered by earthquakes, melting snow, human activity, or other factors. You can help protect yourself and those you are traveling with by being alert, staying on the trail, and avoiding being directly underneath or above other hikers. If you see a falling rock, yell "ROCK" at the top of your lungs to alert other hikers as quickly as possible to the potential threat. If you're hiking in or near a riverbed and the water turns from clear to muddy or the water level begins to rise quickly, get to high ground immediately as these could be indications of a flash flood further upstream.

Strikes & Government Shutdowns

Another unpredictable yet, fortunately, not so common occurrence is a government shutdown. In 2013, a 16-day federal shutdown forced over 400 national parks to close their gates during the first half of October. During that time, access roads to trailheads and all permit issuing stations were closed. As a precaution, always check to make sure that your public transportation is running as expected and that the park entrance is open before you set off on your trip. In the event of a shutdown, however, there is nothing you can do besides adjusting your travel plans.

* * *

Figure 9 – Approaching Evolution Lake

4. Long Lead Items

Arranging a multi-day backpacking trip on the JMT involves several steps. Some of these steps require more lead time than others. This chapter introduces the most important items that require advance thinking and preparation in order to have a successful and enjoyable journey.

a. Permits

Along the entire JMT corridor, a valid permit is required for all overnight wilderness use. Despite passing through five separate jurisdictions, one permit can be valid for the entire 221-mile route as the result of an interagency agreement. The process of obtaining the wilderness permit, however, may be different depending on where (i.e., in which jurisdiction) you intend to start your hike. Permit holders must know and obey all wilderness regulations and area-specific restrictions (as outlined in Section 3a *Trails & Navigation*).

! The issued wilderness permit must be in your possession at all times, and you cannot leave the wilderness for more than 24 hours, or else your permit may be become invalid.

In order to preserve the wilderness and restrict trail use, trailhead quotas have been put in place to limit the number of hikers allowed to enter a particular area the same day. Different trailheads can have different quotas, and advance permit reservations may be available. Each jurisdiction has its own key dates and procedures for accepting and processing applications (as shown in Table 6 below). In order to cope with the tremendous demand for permits at both ends of the JMT, Yosemite NP and Whitney Portal (Inyo NF) were forced to implement lottery systems.

Differentiator	Yosemite NP	Whitney Portal (Inyo NF)	Inyo NF	Sierra NF	SEKI NP
Quota Period	May - Oct	May 1 - Nov 1	May 1 - Nov 1	Year-round	May - Sep
Daily Quota	45 (Donohue Exit)	60 (Overnight)	Varies by trailhead	Varies by trailhead	Varies by trailhead
Reservable Quota	35	60	60% of available permits	60% of available permits	75% of available permits
When to Reserve	24 weeks (168 days) in advance	February 1 - March 15	6 months in advance	1 year in advance	March 1
How to Reserve	Fax (best), phone, mail	Web (recreation.gov)	Web (recreation.gov)	Mail	Fax (best), mail
Processing Order	Daily lottery	One-time lottery	In order received	In order received	In order received
Reservation Fees	$5/reservation, plus $5/person	$6/reservation, plus $15/person	$6/res., plus $5/p. ($15/p. if Whitney Zone)	$5/person ($15/person if Whitney Zone)	$10/reservation, plus $5/person
Walk-up Permits (earliest avail.)	11:00 AM the day before entry date	11:00 AM the day before entry date	11:00 AM the day before entry date	24 hours prior to entry date	1:00 PM the day before entry date

Table 6 – Permit Options based on Entry Points

The main pros and cons of each hiking direction (NOBO/SOBO/MOBO) have already been discussed in Section 3a *Trails & Navigation*. The following overview of permit-related considerations will help you further refine your decision on where to start your JMT adventure and manage your overall expectations.

For most current information on permit quotas, application procedures, and associated fees, refer to each jurisdiction's respective website.

Hiking SOBO, starting in Yosemite National Park

Yosemite, without a doubt, is the number one starting point choice of many prospective JMT hikers. As a result, you can expect to compete with multitudes of highly-motivated people over the limited supply of permits. Patience and flexibility will be key to increasing your chances of success.

Trailhead Options

Starting your JMT thru-hike in Yosemite National Park, you have four trailheads to choose from: Happy Isles and Glacier Point in Yosemite Valley as well as Sunrise Lakes and Lyell Canyon in Tuolumne Meadows.

Happy Isles

Marking the official northern terminus of the JMT, Happy Isles is by far the most popular trailhead and, consequently, the most competitive in terms of permits. Starting at 4,000 feet (1,220m), you'll have a tough but very scenic first day, gaining over 2,000 feet (610m) in elevation while passing some of Yosemite's most iconic landmarks, including Vernal Falls, Nevada Falls, and Half Dome. For your permit, you will need to decide whether to spend your first night camping at Little Yosemite Valley (LYV) or to "pass through" to Sunrise/Merced Lake, camping somewhere along Sunrise Creek past the Clouds Rest Trail junction. Both of these locations will be busy, so the deciding factor should be how many miles you'll want to cover on day 1.

Glacier Point

Starting at Glacier Point, your first 5.6 miles (9km) will take you along the Panorama Trail past Illilouette Falls, with outstanding views of Vernal and Nevada Falls as well as Half Dome. To get to the trailhead, you can choose to hike up the steep Four-Mile Trail from the valley floor (4.7 miles, 3,200 ft. gain) or take the hiker's bus from Yosemite Valley Lodge ($25 one-way, reservation recommended). From there, it will be much more pleasant hiking compared to the strenuous climb out of Happy Isles. The Panorama Trail joins the JMT just before Nevada Falls. Your designated campsite for the first night will be Little Yosemite Valley.

Sunrise Lakes

Sunrise Lakes Trailhead is located at Tenaya Lake on Tioga Pass Road, just a short drive from Tuolumne Meadows. Starting here, the 4.8-mile (7.7km) Sunrise Lakes Trail follows a gradual incline until joining the JMT at SOBO mile 13.4 near the Sunrise High Sierra Camp, which is where you'll be able to set up camp the first night. Although this option has you skip Yosemite Valley altogether, there are some advantages worth considering. First, you can park your car at Tuolumne Meadows and take the free shuttle to Sunrise Lakes, allowing you to pass by your car a few days later to drop off gear items or resupply food as needed. Second, from Sunrise Lakes, you'll have direct access to the Clouds Rest Trail, allowing you to include a side trip to the 9,926-foot (3,025m) granite peak to enjoy incredible 360-degree panoramic views of Yosemite, including Half Dome.

Lyell Canyon

Located next to the Tuolumne Meadows Wilderness Center, Lyell Canyon Trailhead provides quick access to the JMT near SOBO mile 23.8 via a short spur trail. The main reasons for choosing this entry point include the slightly less competitive permit process (even walk-up permits are available) and the relatively flat terrain through Lyell Canyon on day 1. A popular choice for the first night's campsite is the area near the Lyell Fork Footbridge. The major downside of starting at Lyell Canyon is missing out on some of Yosemite's most spectacular scenery. If this is a concern, consider shuttling to Yosemite Valley a few days prior to your Lyell Canyon start date and either apply for a walk-up wilderness permit to get to Tuolumne Meadows or, as a last resort, to day-hike the 22-mile (35km) stretch, which does not require a permit.

Permit Availability

Yosemite's quota period is May through October. For trips starting during that time, a total of 100 JMT wilderness permits are available per day for the above-listed trailheads. Of these permits, 60% can be reserved in advance, with 40% remaining as walk-up permits. However, in 2015, the NPS introduced a supplemental quota to limit the number of hikers exiting Yosemite NP over Donohue Pass, effectively reducing the total number of available JMT permits to 45 per day (see Table 7 below for details). The exit quota was implemented on an interim basis to preserve the quality of JMT experience and to balance the number of permits issued to hikers passing through Yosemite and those staying within the park.

<table>
<tr><th rowspan="2">Trailhead</th><th colspan="2">Total Quota</th><th colspan="2">Donohue Exit</th></tr>
<tr><th>Reservable</th><th>Walk-up</th><th>Reservable</th><th>Walk-up</th></tr>
<tr><td>Happy Isles → Little Yos. Valley</td><td>18</td><td>12</td><td rowspan="4">20</td><td rowspan="4">-</td></tr>
<tr><td>Happy Isles → Sunrise/Merced</td><td>6</td><td>4</td></tr>
<tr><td>Glacier Point → Little Yos. Valley</td><td>6</td><td>4</td></tr>
<tr><td>Sunrise Lakes (Tuolum. Mdw.)</td><td>9</td><td>6</td></tr>
<tr><td>Lyell Canyon (Tuolum. Mdw.)</td><td>21</td><td>14</td><td>15</td><td>10</td></tr>
<tr><td>Total</td><td>60</td><td>40</td><td>35</td><td>10</td></tr>
</table>

Table 7 – Yosemite Trailhead Quotas

To put the 35 reservable Donohue Exit permits in perspective, Figure 10 shows Yosemite wilderness permit application data for 2016. For trips starting during main season, the permit office received an average of 300-500 advance reservation requests per day (peaking near 700 on busy days). Although the data represents permit requests received for all of Yosemite, it is reasonable to assume that 80-90% of them are for the JMT. Keeping in mind that one request can include multiple people, it is not surprising that the NPS/YOSE website states that over 97% of JMT thru-hike permit requests for Yosemite Valley have to be denied. While this is certainly a sobering realization, it should not discourage anyone from pursuing their dream of hiking the JMT, especially given the numerous alternatives presented in the remainder of this chapter.

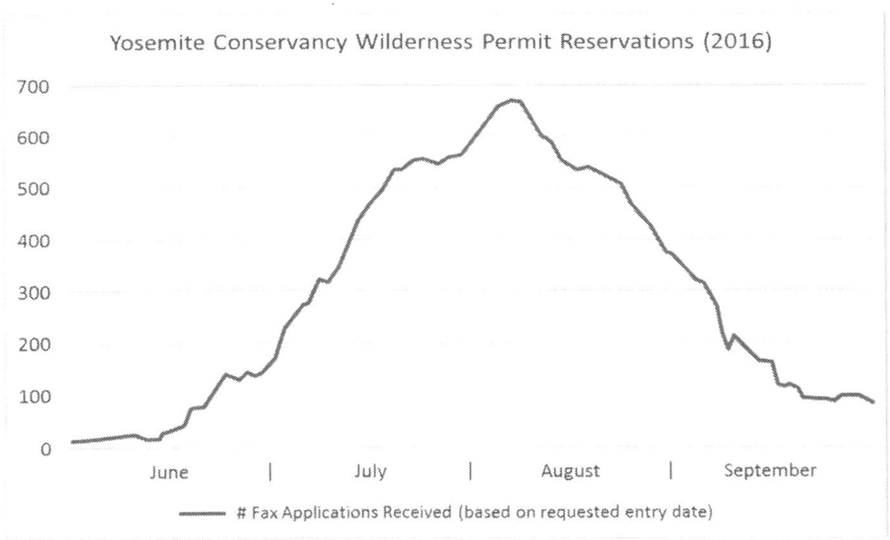

Source: https://www.nps.gov/yose/planyourvisit/wpres.htm

Figure 10 – Wilderness Permit Reservation Faxes Received (2016)

Application Process

All advance permits become available 24 weeks (168 days) prior to the actual start date, and reservation requests can be made via fax, phone, or mail. Faxing is undeniably the best method, since applications can be submitted as early as 12:01 AM PST the day before permits become available. All faxes received until 7:30 AM PST on day 168 will be processed as part of a lottery. Phone reservations and all other request will be processed in the order received only after the fax lottery is done. In order to assist hikers with identifying the correct advance submission date(s), the NPS/YOSE website provides a complete schedule of available entry dates and their respective submission and processing deadlines. See Table 8 below for a few examples from the official schedule.

Intended Start Date	First Day to Fax	Date Faxes Processed	First Day to Call
June1	December 14	December 15	December 15
July 1	January 13	January 14	January 14
August 1	February 13	February 14	February 14
...	...	...	...

Source: https://www.nps.gov/yose/planyourvisit/wildpermitdates.htm

Table 8 – Earliest Submission Dates based on Start Date (Samples)

Example: Assuming your intended start date is July 1, then your permit request will be processed as part of the lottery on January 14. In order to participate in the lottery, you need to submit your fax application between 12:01 AM PST on January 13 and 7:30 AM PST on January 14.

[!] Given the ever-increasing demand, it can be assumed that all available permits will be allocated as part of the lottery. Therefore, it is crucial not to miss the 31.5-hour early fax submission window!

In preparation for your submission, download the *Yosemite National Park Wilderness Permit Reservation Application* form (available as PDF on NPS/YOSE website), and fill it out carefully, following the step-by-step instructions provided on the website. Completing the form is relatively straightforward, but one thing folks occasionally struggle with is filling in the first night's camp location in the wilderness. Unless your trailhead selection designates a specific camping site (e.g., Happy Isles → Little Yosemite Valley), you can pick any location as long as it is permissible per wilderness regulations. To get you started, Table 9 below lists designated/ possible campsites for each of the four JMT entry trailheads.

Entry Trailhead	First Night Camp
Happy Isles → Little Yosemite Valley	Little Yosemite Valley (LYV)
Happy Isles → Sunrise/Merced Lake Pass Through	Clouds Rest Trail junction
Glacier Point → Little Yosemite Valley	Little Yosemite Valley (LYV)
Sunrise Lakes (Tenaya Lake South)	Sunrise Camp
Lyell Canyon	Lyell Fork Footbridge

Table 9 – Designated/Possible First Night Camps based on Entry Trailhead

For most people, the exit trailhead will be Whitney Portal, which includes the option to summit Mt. Whitney. Although you are asked to provide realistic estimates, both exit trailhead and exit date are non-binding and can be changed at a later time without penalty. To facilitate processing, it is recommended to fill out the form using a computer rather than by hand. Be sure to include a valid email address with your request to receive a notification with your lottery results within 24-48 hours of the processing date. If your permit request is confirmed, a non-refundable fee of $5 for the reservation plus $5 per person is charged using the provided payment method. If your reservation request is denied, you will not be charged.

Permit Pickup

If you receive a notification that your advance reservation was successful, be aware that this is not your permit. You, or another member of your hiking group, must still pick up the actual wilderness permit at a permit-issuing station (e.g., Wilderness Center in Yosemite Valley or Tuolumne Meadows) during business hours the day of or the day before your hike. Reserved permits are held until 10:00 AM on the day of your trip. If you anticipate to arrive later than 10:00 AM, call +1 (209) 372-0308 ahead of time to notify park staff, otherwise your reservation will be canceled. Permits held for late arrival must still be picked up during business hours.

ⓘ Wilderness permit holders are allowed to spend the night before and after a wilderness trip in one of Yosemite's designated backpackers' campgrounds (see Section 4d *Accommodation* for details).

If your advance reservation was not successful, consider getting a first-come, first-served permit at the permit-issuing station closest to your desired entry point. For the 10 available Lyell Canyon permits, this would be the Tuolumne Meadows Wilderness Center. First-come, first-served permits become available at 11:00 AM the day prior to your planned departure. You may even be so lucky to pick up a permit that becomes available due to a cancelled reservation on the same day. However, in order to snatch one of these last-minute tickets, be prepared to get in line early (camping/sleeping in front of wilderness centers is not allowed)!

Permit Strategies

If you're determined to start your hike in Yosemite despite the unfavorable odds, the following strategies will help increase your likelihood of success:

<u>Keep your group size small</u>

Since the quota regulates the number of people who can access the trail, not the number of permits given out, you can increase your chances by keeping the number of people on your permit to a minimum. Logically, applying as only one person will have the best chances. However, if you'd prefer to hike as a group, the application form gives you the option to specify the *Minimum Number of People Acceptable*. As an example, let's say you are a group of four who are interested in hiking the JMT, but only two are able to fully commit at the time the application window opens. Then, you can try to get a permit for everyone by entering a '4' for *Number of People* but are well-advised to also enter a '2' for *Minimum Number of People Acceptable*.

<u>Be flexible with entry dates & entry points</u>

Your ideal application should list three different entry trailheads for the same entry date, since reservation requests are processed one day at a time as part of the permit lottery. Happy Isles, Glacier Point, and Sunrise Lakes are lumped together with regards to the Donohue Pass exit quota, so to increase your chances, be sure to include Lyell Canyon as one of your choices. Choosing dates that fall in the shoulder season (May/June,

September/October) will further improve your odds (weather will be more inclement however). Keep submitting your application daily until you get a confirmation, or until your window of opportunity closes. In the unlikely event that you receive multiple confirmations, you can (and should) simply cancel any unwanted dates, making someone else happy down the line. Be aware that you're not allowed to send the same request multiple times per day per group. Duplicate applications compromise the fairness of the process and create a lot of additional effort. Thus, they will be excluded from the lottery and are subject to a non-refundable fee.

Keep an eye out for cancelled reservations

If all advance reservation attempts have failed, don't despair just yet. It is not uncommon for spaces to open up throughout the season due to cancellations. The wilderness permit staff maintains a *Full Trailheads Report* (which is available on the NPS/YOSE website) that includes details on available quotas for each of the five JMT entry trailhead options, taking into account the Donohue Exit Quota. The report is updated constantly, so be sure to monitor closely and act quickly if a space opens up.

Hiking NOBO, starting at Whitney Portal

The 14,505-foot summit of Mt. Whitney marks the official southern terminus of the JMT. For backpackers, the shortest way to get there is the 10.7-mile trail leading up from Whitney Portal. Every year, more and more hikers consider a northbound JMT itinerary in hopes of better chances of reserving a permit. However, getting an overnight wilderness permit to start at Whitney Portal is only slightly less competitive than Yosemite. Mt. Whitney itself as well as the adjacent Sequoia National Park attract their own hordes of backpacking enthusiasts, with which you will be competing.

Trailhead Options

Whitney Portal is one of many trailheads in Inyo NF. However, the fact that it is the closest trailhead to Mt. Whitney puts it in a unique position. Similar to Yosemite, the demand for Whitney Portal permits significantly exceeds the available quota. As a result, a lottery system is used as well.

Permit Availability

Inyo Nation Forest trailhead quotas apply from May 1 to November 1. There are no quotas during the rest of the year, however, permits are still required. To start your JMT trip at Whitney Portal, you will need a *Mt. Whitney Trail Overnight* permit. During the quota period, 60 of these permits are available per day and 100% of them can be reserved in advance, either as part of the lottery or thereafter (although the quota is typically filled by the lottery). Additional openings may become available at a later time due to cancellations.

On their website, the Inyo National Forest wilderness permit office provides a comprehensive *Mt. Whitney Lottery Results* report, which includes very detailed statistics on overnight permit applications. In 2015, for instance, 7,024 applications were submitted, requesting overnight permits for a total of 33,211 people during the JMT peak season (June to September). Taking into account the available 7,320 permits for that time period (= 60 permits/day x 122 days) leads to a theoretical average chance of success of about 22%.

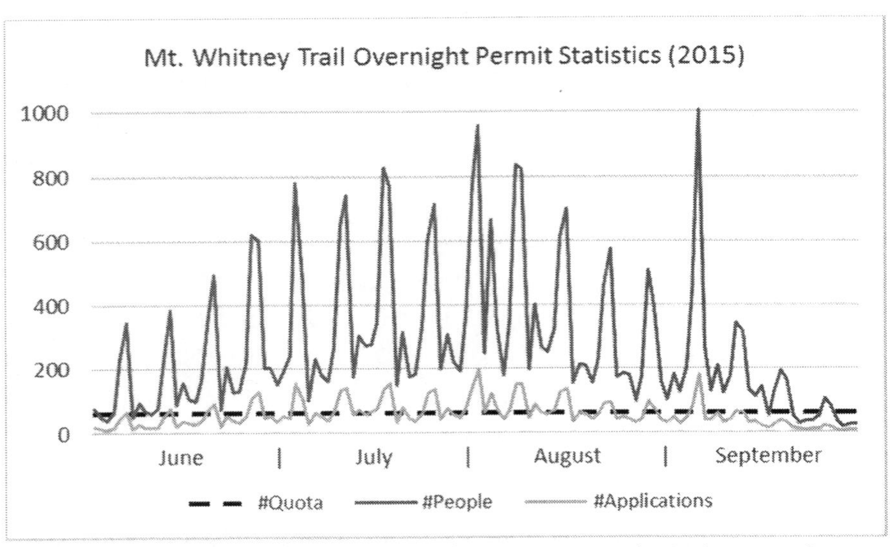

Source: http://www.fs.usda.gov/Internet/FSE_DOCUMENTS/stelprd3829478.docx

Figure 11 – Overnight Permit Applications Received (2015)

In reality, there is a lot more variance (as shown in Figure 11 above) depending on the day of the week you want to enter the trail. Fridays and Saturdays are extremely popular, reducing the average chance of success to 11%, whereas the odds for Sunday through Thursday average at 35%.

Application Process

Overnight permits can be reserved via *Recreation.gov* (search for "Inyo National Forest - Wilderness Permits"), requiring you to create an account. Reservations include a non-refundable $6/group transaction fee, plus a $15/person reservation fee. In order to participate in the annual lottery, you need to submit your application between February 1 and March 15 (midnight Eastern Time). All requests received during that time period are then processed together in one lottery. Starting March 24, all participants can preview the lottery results by logging into their Recreation.gov account. Any spaces not reserved as part of the lottery will become available to the general public on April 1. Further online reservations can be made until two days before the trip.

Permit Acceptance

As an additional step, you will need to accept any date you won in the lottery between April 1 and April 30. Your reservation is not final until you complete your purchase online and pay the reservation fees in full. If this is not done before midnight Eastern Time on April 30, the reservation will be canceled. On May 1, all remaining unclaimed dates are canceled and returned to the reservation calendar within 24 hours (at random times).

While some changes (itinerary, exit date) can be made to existing reservations, they cannot be sold or transferred to other parties.

Permit Pickup

The group leader or alternate leader can check in at the Eastern Sierra Interagency Visitor Center in Lone Pine and pick up the wilderness permit as early as two days before the entry date. However, the permit must be picked up before 10:00 AM PDT on the entry date, otherwise, the reservation will be cancelled as a no-show. Alternatively, you can confirm your group size up to 14 days before the trip, which will prevent the no-show and extend your pickup window until close of business on the trip entry date. If checking in during business hours is no option at all, you can arrange for your permit to be placed in a night box, which is located outside the visitor center. However, you must call the visitor center staff at +1 (760) 873-2483 a few days before your trip to request this service, since it will not happen automatically.

Eastern Sierra Interagency Visitor Center
Jct. of US-395 & CA-136
Lone Pine, CA 93545
Phone: +1 (760) 876-6222

If you missed the lottery window and weren't able to reserve a spot otherwise, you can try to obtain a walk-up permit directly from the visitor center (in person only, no online or phone orders). During the quota season, visitor center staffs starts issuing walk-up permits for same day entry at 8:00 AM each day. At 11:00 AM, no-shows for the same day entry as well as walk-up permits for next day entry become available.

Permit Strategies

If you're determined to start your hike at Whitney Portal despite the fierce competition, the following tips will help increase your chances of success:

Keep your group size small

Similar to Yosemite, the Mt. Whitney Trail quota determines the number of people who are granted access, not the number of permits given out. Therefore, you can increase your chances of "winning" the lottery by keeping the number of people on your application small. Be aware that the lottery limits participants to one application per group and trip. Groups that submit multiple applications for the same dates are subject to applications being rejected. If you wish to reserve multiple trips in the same year, you are allowed to do so after the April 1 cut-off date, when unreserved spaces are being released.

Be flexible with entry dates & entry points

As part of your lottery application, you have the option to select as many as 15 different entry dates. Take advantage of that if your schedule allows. In addition, choosing less popular dates (Sun-Thu, shoulder season) will further increase the likelihood of success. If your schedule is rather limited, consider starting your trip from one of the more distant trailheads, like Kearsarge Pass (Onion Valley) or Cottonwood Pass (Horseshoe Meadow), which are not part of the lottery. Permits for these trails can be reserved online up to six months in advance (see "Hiking MOBO" section below).

Keep an eye out for unreserved spaces

If your lottery reservation request was unsuccessful or you missed the application window altogether, your next best option to is to go online and try to make a reservation after unreserved spaces become available on April 1. The Recreation.gov website features a reservation calendar which shows available date ranges (indicated by letter 'A') and fully-reserved dates (letter 'R').

Hiking MOBO, starting somewhere in between

While Yosemite and Mt. Whitney represent the official ending points of the JMT, their increasingly competitive permit lotteries have inspired hikers to come up with modified itineraries, utilizing different entry points to access and complete the JMT. If you're willing to put in the extra effort for the logistics, you can begin your trip somewhere in the middle, then hike either north to Happy Isles or south to Mt. Whitney, then return to the middle, and complete the remaining portion of the trail in the opposite direction (also known as 'flip-flop'). Inyo NF, Sierra NF, and SEKI offer a range of alternative entry trailheads, and obtaining the required permits is much more straightforward.

Inyo National Forest

There are several trailheads in Inyo National Forest you can start your modified JMT experience from. Go to *Recreation.gov* and search for "Inyo

National Forest - Wilderness Permits" to view the complete list of available options. The website is very straightforward and is also used to make reservations. Between May 1 and November 1 (same as Whitney Portal), trailheads are subject to daily quotas. For most trails, 60% of the available permits can be reserved online up to six months in advance without any lottery – the main exception being Whitney Portal. The remaining 40% of permits can be requested on a walk-up basis.

Recommended Trailheads: Rush Creek, JMT North of Devils Postpile, JMT South of Devils Postpile, Piute Pass, Bishop Pass, Kearsarge Pass, Cottonwood Pass (see Table 1 on page 14 for details)

Permit Options

Inyo National Forest issues different types of permits depending on the nature of your trip, your intention to visit the Whitney Zone, and any plans to exit the wilderness via Whitney Portal. The following options are available:

- *Overnight* – Choose this option to enter the JMT from any Inyo NF trailhead (except Whitney Portal). If you plan to summit Mt. Whitney from the west via Guitar Lake and return to the JMT the same way, this permit will suffice since the peak is located in SEKI, outside the boundaries of the Whitney Zone.
- *Overnight Visiting Mt. Whitney* – Choose this option if you intend to enter the Whitney Zone but don't plan to exit the JMT via Trail Crest to finish your trip at Whitney Portal.
- *Overnight Exiting Mt. Whitney* – Choose this option if you plan to exit the JMT via Trail Crest to finish your trip at Whitney Portal. Note, this permit is subject to the Trail Crest Exit Quota (see details below) and thus more difficult to get.
- *Cross Country (Visiting/Exiting Mt. Whitney)* – This type of permit is needed for all off-trail exploring in Inyo NF. JMT hikers typically don't choose this option, since they're traveling on established trails only, for which overnight permits are sufficient.

Trail Crest Exit Quota

The Trail Crest Exit Quota is 25 people per day. It applies to all visitors who start their trip within Inyo National Forest and plan to descend the Mt. Whitney Trail in order to finish at Whitney Portal. If you begin your hike outside of Inyo NF and your JMT permit states that you are exiting at Mt. Whitney, then you *are not* subject to the Trail Crest Exit Quota.

Reservation Process & Pickup

As part of the permit reservation via Recreation.gov, you will be required to provide specific details in terms of permit type needed, entry trailhead, entry date, group size, preliminary itinerary (incl. campsites), and exit date (if you plan to finish at Whitney Portal). In order to facilitate this process, it is best to map out your trip before going online to fill out the forms. If you're unsure about your entry point, have a look at Table 1 on page 14 which includes a list of Inyo National Forest trailheads that provide convenient access to the JMT. The entry trailhead, entry date, and exit date (if subject to exit quota) you specify for your permit are binding. The campsites you select for your itinerary should be reasonable, but they're not binding. The information is useful to locate hikers in case of emergency.

Permit reservations include a transaction fee of $6 per group, plus a $5 per person fee ($15/person if Visiting/Exiting Mt. Whitney). The instructions for picking up your permit are essentially the same as described in the 'Hiking NOBO' section above, except you can go to any of the following Inyo NF permit issuing stations (be sure to check individual business hours):

- *Easter Sierra Interagency Visitor Center (Lone Pine, CA)*
- *White Mountain Ranger Station (Bishop, CA)*
- *Mammoth Lakes Welcome Center (Mammoth Lakes, CA)*
- *Mono Basin Scenic Area Visitor Center (Lee Vining, CA)*

Sierra National Forest

Sierra National Forest has a few trailheads that lend themselves as good starting points for a modified JMT itinerary. For a list of available options, go to *http://www.fs.usda.gov/detail/sierra/*. Trailhead quotas are in place year-round, and 60% of the permits can be reserved up to one year in advance (min. 21 days before entry) by submitting an application form via mail. The remaining 40% of permits can be requested on a walk-up basis.

Recommended Trailheads: Mono Creek, Florence Lake (see Table 1 on page 14 for details)

Reservation Process & Pickup

In order to reserve a permit, download the *Wilderness Permit Reservation Application* form from the Sierra National Forest website and follow the instructions included in the document. You will be required to provide specific details on your group size, entry/exit dates, entry/exit trails, and your preliminary itinerary (incl. campsites). The completed form then needs to be mailed to either the Bass Lake Ranger District or the High Sierra Ranger District, depending on entry trailhead. For Mono Creek and Florence Lake it is the latter location.

High Sierra Ranger District
Attn: Wilderness Permits
P.O. Box 559
Prather CA, 93651
Phone: +1 (559) 855-5355 ext. 0

Permit reservations require a $5 per person fee ($15/person if exiting via Mt. Whitney). The payment needs to be included in your initial submission. If your request is successful, you will receive a confirmation letter of your reservation by mail. If your request cannot be filled, your application and fees will be returned. The confirmation letter is not your permit, however, it will indicate the location where you can pick up your permit up to 48 hours before your entry date. Permits must be picked up in person by 12:00 PM on the day of the departure, or they will be re-issued to another party. There is a $10.00 fee for changes to a confirmed reservation. Walk-up permits are available 24 hours prior to the intended entry date at no charge.

Sequoia and Kings Canyon National Park

Accessing the JMT via SEKI trailheads is a possibility, although it may not be as convenient compared to many of the above-listed options. Go to the NPS/SEKI website to learn more about available entry trailheads. Daily quotas apply between end of May and end of September (actual dates vary annually). There are no quotas during the rest of the year, however, permits are still required (free, self-issued). For trips within the quota period, approximately 75% of the available permits can be reserved in advance, starting at 12:01 AM PST on March 1 each year, by submitting an application form either by fax or mail. The remaining 25% of permits are issued on a first-come, first-served basis.

Recommended Trailhead: Bubb's Creek (see Table 1 on page 14 for details)

Application Process & Pickup

In order to reserve a permit, download the *Wilderness Permit Application* form from the NPS/SEKI website and follow the instructions included in the document. You will be required to provide specific details on your entry/exit dates, entry/exit trails, and your group size. The completed form then needs to be faxed (recommended) or mailed to the SEKI Wilderness Permit Reservation Office, but no sooner than 12:01 AM PST on March 1. No reservations over the phone or by email. Applications received prior to March 1 will not be processed.

Wilderness Permit Reservations
47050 Generals Hwy #60
Three Rivers, CA 93271
Phone: +1 (559) 565-3766
Email: seki_wilderness_office@nps.gov

Reservations require a payment of $10 per permit, plus $5 per person. The payment needs to be included in your initial submission (credit card accepted as well). Fees are non-refundable once a permit request has been approved. The Wilderness Office processes applications in the order they are received. All applicants will receive an email response within two weeks. If your request cannot be filled, you won't be charged. The confirmation email is not your permit, however, it will include details on where to pick up your permit. Permits must be picked up in person at the designated ranger station during normal business hours (there are no night boxes). For Bubb's Creek trailhead it is the Road's End Permit Station. You can pick up your permit (incl. walk-ups) as early as 1:00 PM the day before your trip but no later than 9:00 AM on the day of your entry date. If you need to arrange for a late pick up, call or email the Wilderness Office. After 9:00 AM, any unclaimed reservations will be cancelled and released as walk-up permits.

Permit Strategies

Getting a SEKI wilderness permit is not quite as competitive (yet) as the lotteries for Yosemite and Whitney Portal. Nevertheless, the below tips will help maximize your chances of getting a permit for the days and size of group you are requesting:

Submit promptly

Ideally, you want to submit your application promptly after reservations open at 12:01 AM PST on March 1. The longer you wait, the more likely that permits will no longer be available for your preferred days. Quotas for popular days (weekends/holidays) and peak season (summer months) can fill up quickly. Be sure to submit your request via fax, since applications are processed in the order received.

Keep your group size small

The smaller your group size, the more likely that there will still be spots for you. Similar to Yosemite, the SEKI application form gives you the option to specify the *Minimum Number of People Acceptable* in addition to the *Preferred Number of People*. If there are any uncertain candidates in your group, it is recommended to make use of this option.

Provide multiple alternative entry dates

The permit application allows you to choose up to four alternatives for entry dates and trails. Take advantage of tis if your schedule allows. Wilderness Office staff will issue your permit for the first day that is available based on the order you list your choices. Do not submit multiple applications with same entry date and trailhead combinations per group. Duplicate requests slow down the process and may result in duplicate, non-refundable charges.

Keep an eye out for unreserved spaces & cancellations

If your initial permit request was unsuccessful or you weren't able to submit early on, you can check the NPS/SEKI website for unreserved spaces. Simply search for "Wilderness Permit Reservation Availability", and you'll get the full list of SEKI trailheads and their available quota.

ⓘ Although it adds 50+ miles (80+ km) to the overall mileage, some folks choose to access the JMT via the High Sierra Trail, starting at the Crescent Meadow trailhead in SEKI. It's a remarkable route that traverses the Sierra Nevada west to east for the most part, before merging with the JMT near Wallace Creek (SOBO mile 199). For more details on the HST and related planning aspects, check out the *Plan & Go | High Sierra Trail* guidebook (Sandiburg Press 2016).

b. Hiking Buddy

The decision to hike the JMT or any other long-distance trail solo, with a hiking partner, or even as a group may be driven by practical considerations, financial implications, safety concerns, or simply personal preference. Especially, if this is your first multi-day hike, a friend by your side can help navigate through unfamiliar terrain, deal with unexpected obstacles, and keep spirits up as energy levels fade.

Finding the right companion can be a challenging endeavor in itself and should be given thorough thought. The following questions may aid you in your decision-making process when looking for potential candidates:

- Will you be comfortable being around that person 24/7 for the entire duration of your trip?
- Do all of you have somewhat similar fitness levels and hiking experience?
- Do all of you share similar interests and expectations (e.g., taking lots of photos, off-trail relaxing/exploring)?

If you decide to look for a hiking partner, approach people early, so they have sufficient time to carefully assess the challenge at hand and whether or not they have the required resources. Potential doubts and concerns should be discussed openly and sorted out well before hitting the trail.

With regard to gear and supplies, traveling alone or with others can make a difference, but not necessarily a big one. Usually, you can share a stove, pot, water purifier, first aid kit, pocket knife, emergency rope, map, shovel, and a camera. These items can add up to approximately 4 lbs. (1.8kg). Sharing that weight with one person would save each of you 2 lbs. (0.9kg) and in a group of four, the individual pack weight would be reduced by 3 lbs. (1.4kg). Sharing other gear items may be more difficult or simply undesirable. Sharing a tent, for example, could potentially save additional weight. However, being able to retreat into your own shelter after a long day of hiking may be well worth carrying a few extra pounds.

In case of emergency, it is obviously good to have someone close-by. Although the JMT is well-frequented in the summer time, you never know when another hiker will pass. For several other reasons, it is wonderful to bring a companion. You have someone to chat with, discuss spontaneous ideas, indulge in philosophical ramblings, and share other sun-ripened strokes of genius when no other human is in sight. Recalling the stunning scenery and imposing wildlife you saw during the day while waiting for the water to boil at camp will help engrave those impressions even deeper into your brain. Ultimately, the shared memories will stay with you for life.

However, it may not always be possible to find a hiking buddy for a particular trip, or you could just decide to venture off on your own to test your physical abilities and mental strength while experiencing absolute solitude. Hiking the JMT alone is a viable option and quite common. Carrying the necessary gear and supplies by yourself is absolutely manageable. If you intend to start alone but hope to join/form a group along the way, then hiking the in the popular north-to-south direction will greatly increase your chances.

c. Travel Arrangements

Getting to and from the main trailheads at Yosemite Valley and Whitney Portal takes some planning but is still rather convenient considering the fact that you are entering a wilderness zone. Depending on where you are coming from and which direction you intend to walk the JMT, there are several options to choose from. Figure 12 below provides an overview of major towns and traffic routes near the trail as well as airport connections and car rental locations.

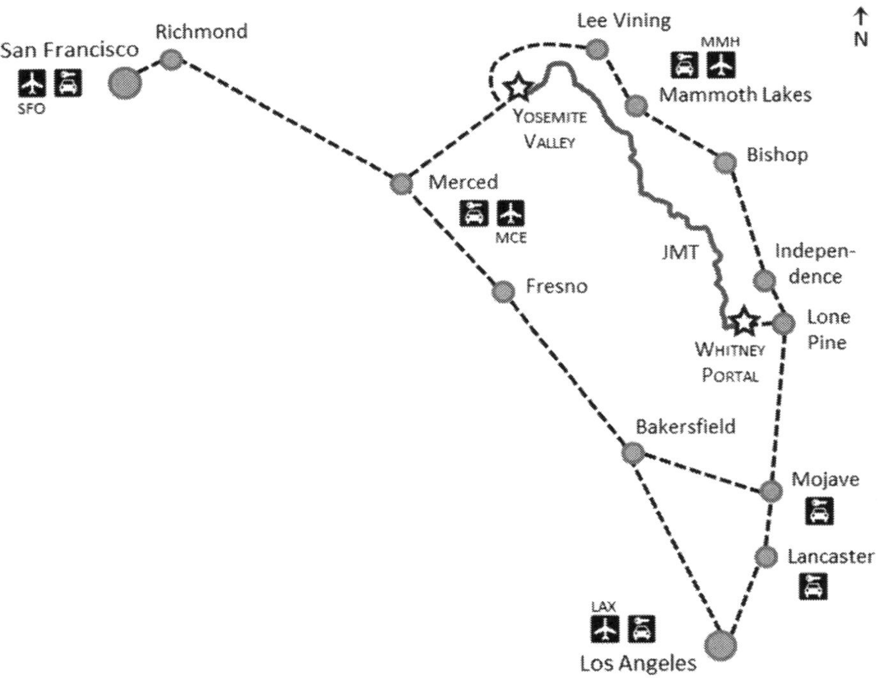

Figure 12 – Overview Map of Travel Options

Drop-off and Pickup by Family and Friends

If you can arrange it, this is probably the most convenient and flexible option for getting to and from the JMT. It eliminates the need for dropping off and retrieving cars before and after your trip as well as the hassle of having to coordinate public transportation. Maybe you have a family member or friend who is willing to do it for free or for gas money. Even if it takes a bit more "incentive" to get them to agree, it's worth it.

Personal Car & Parking

Both Yosemite Valley and Whitney Portal offer long-term parking, giving you the option to leave a car at one trailhead, and then use public transportation to get to the other. Since it can be hard to predict exactly what time, or even day, you will finish your hike, leaving your car at the ending trailhead gives you flexibility to immediately start your trip home or head into town to stay for the night.

[!] Since you *must be on time* to pick up your permit, if you decide to leave your car at the ending trailhead, make sure you understand how you are going to get to the permit office and how long it is going to take you.

There is bear activity at both trailheads, which means that you should not leave any food or scented items in your car. If you absolutely have to, at least make sure you cover up any food and/or coolers or store them in the trunk so that they are not visible to bears. This will minimize the likelihood of coming back to a bear-induced crime scene of mangled auto parts and food wrappers.

(i) As a precaution, it is advisable to leave a note on your car dashboard indicating the starting date of the trip, the trail you will be on, and the expected return date. This serves two purposes: First, park rangers will know that your car will be there for a while, and second, if the expected return date has come and gone and the car is still there, it can alert them that you could be in trouble.

If there is not enough room in the Whitney Portal parking lot, there are several long-term parking options in Lone Pine that you can contact, including the Film History Museum, the Chamber of Commerce, the Golf Course, and the Dow Villa Motel.

Public Transportation

Amtrak

Major railroad carrier in California used for long trips between cities. You can take this carrier to get from Los Angeles or San Francisco to the city of Merced (and vice versa).

Website: *http://www.amtrak.com*

Bay Area Rapid Transit (BART)

Regional rail service that will take you from San Francisco International Airport (SFO) to the city of Richmond, CA, where you can link up with Amtrak trains for longer distance travel throughout California.

Website: *http://www.bart.gov*

Eastern Sierra Transit Authority (ESTA)

Bus service traveling along Highway 395. You can use ESTA to go north or south from the city of Lone Pine, CA, which is located approx. 11 miles from the trailhead at Whitney Portal. The bus runs only on certain days of the week, so be sure to check the current schedule.

Website: *http://www.estransit.com*

FlyAway Bus

Bus services that will take you to and from Los Angeles International Airport (LAX) and Union Station, the major train station in Los Angeles. You will need to print your reservation and bring it with you. Tickets are valid for 30 days after the date of purchase.

Website: *http://www.lawa.org/FlyAway/*

Megabus

Long-distance bus service. Megabus can transport you between Los Angeles and San Francisco and is generally less expensive than traveling by train, however, route options are limited.

Website: *http://us.megabus.com*

Metrolink

Regional passenger rail system serving Southern California. You can take this carrier to get from the city of Lancaster to Los Angeles (and vice versa).

Website: h*ttp://www.metrolinktrains.com*

Yosemite Area Regional Transportation System (YARTS)

YARTS is public transit in the Yosemite region, with buses entering Yosemite Valley from Merced, Mammoth Lakes, Sonora, and Fresno – as well as many different towns along the way.

Website: *http://www.yarts.com*

Sample Itineraries

The below sample itineraries show possible connections from the two major hubs (LAX, SFO) to both trailheads and in between, including approximate travel time and cost.

From	To	Transportation	Time	Cost
SFO	Richmond	BART	1h	$10
Richmond	Merced	Amtrak	2.5h	$24
Merced	**Yosemite Valley**	YARTS	2.5h	$13
Total			**6h**	**$47**

Table 10 – Sample Itinerary: SFO to Yosemite Valley

From	To	Transportation	Time	Cost
LAX	L.A. Union Station	FlyAway Bus	1h	$9
L.A. Union St.	Merced	Amtrak	6h	$43
Merced	**Yosemite Valley**	YARTS	2.5h	$13
Total			**9.5h**	**$65**

Table 11 – Sample Itinerary: LAX to Yosemite Valley

From	To	Transport.	Time	Cost
Whitney Portal	Lone Pine	see note below	-	-
Lone Pine	Lancaster	ESTA	3h	$25
Lancaster	L.A. Union Station	Metrolink	2h	$12
L.A. Union Station	West Oakland (BART Station)	Megabus	7h	$20+
West Oakland (BART Station)	**SFO**	BART	1.5h	$10
Total			**13.5h**	**$67+**

Table 12 – Sample Itinerary: Whitney Portal to SFO

From	To	Transportation	Time	Cost
Whitney Portal	Lone Pine	see note below	-	-
Lone Pine	Lancaster	ESTA	3h	$25
Lancaster	L.A. Union Station	Metrolink	2h	$15
L.A. Union St.	**LAX**	FlyAway Bus	1h	$9
Total			**6h**	**$49**

Table 13 – Sample Itinerary: Whitney Portal to LAX

From	To	Transportation	Time	Cost
Whitney Portal	Lone Pine	see note below		-
Lone Pine	Mammoth Lakes	ESTA	2h	$15
Mammoth Lakes	**Yosemite Valley**	YARTS	4h	$18
Total			**6h**	**$33**

Table 14 – Sample Itinerary: Whitney Portal to Yosemite Valley

Note: As of the writing of this book, there is no public transportation available to get from Whitney Portal to the town of Lone Pine 11.4 miles (18.4km) away, which is the nearest point where you will find public transportation. While there are no guarantees, the amount of hikers and campers that are arriving and departing from Whitney Portal means you can probably find someone who would be willing to take you down the mountain to Lone Pine. Whether you are comfortable hitchhiking or not is entirely up to you and should only ever be done with appropriate care and precaution. Alternatively, you could arrange for a private shuttle service or individual to come and pick you up.

Private Shuttle Service/Chartered Transportation

<u>Eastern Sierra Shuttle</u>

This company offers chartered private rides that you can book in advance and customize to your particular needs. Rates depend on the number of people in your party. While not necessarily cheap, this may be your best option for getting from Whitney Portal back to where you will depart for home. You can, for instance, hire them to take you from Whitney Portal back to Lone Pine, the closest connection to public transportation. Contact them to find out more about your options and to make travel reservations.

Website: *http://www.eastsidesierrashuttle.com*

<u>Climber.org</u>

You can check the 'shuttles' section of this online community for additional information about potential transportation options to and from Whitney Portal and other trailheads in the region.

Website: *http://www.climber.org/data/shuttles.html*

<u>Mule Post</u>

You may be able to arrange for a rideshare or alternative transportation on this local classified ads website (similar to Craigslist), which caters to the community of the Eastern Sierra Nevada.

Website: *http://mulepost.com/community/ride-share*

Car Rental

Renting a car can save you a lot of time, in particular if public transportation is inconvenient or simply not available. The car rental centers closest to the trailheads are Merced, Mammoth, Mojave, and Lancaster. Each of these has at least one major car rental agency that offers one-way rentals and is also accessible via bus or train. It is recommended to book your car in advance and check for current office hours.

Regional Airports

Most out-of-state hikers will fly to San Francisco or Los Angeles and then take advantage of any combination of the above buses, trains, and rental cars to complete the last leg to the trail. Alternatively, you could consider flying to one of the regional airports that are closer to the starting and ending trailheads. Merced Regional Airport (MCE) and Mammoth Yosemite Airport (MMH) both have a rental car office on-site. The airport in Merced even has its own YARTS bus stop.

d. Accommodation

There are several established campgrounds near the starting and ending trailheads of the JMT as well as along the route. In addition, there is a number of resorts and special seasonal camps in close proximity of the trail for anyone interested in upgrading their backcountry experience. With the exception of the two designated backpackers' campgrounds (without which the list would not be complete), the below overview focusses on camping and lodging options that require advance planning and reservation.

Yosemite National Park (Northern Terminus)

Yosemite offers a wide range of lodging and camping options. For JMT'ers and other wilderness permit holders, there are designated backpackers' campgrounds available in Yosemite Valley and Tuolumne Meadows to spend the night before and after a wilderness trip (limit one night at a time). The fee is $6 per person, and reservations are not required. There is no parking directly at the campgrounds, but designated overnight parking areas are available in walking distance.

Yosemite Valley Backpackers' Campground	
Location	Behind the North Pines Campground (and across the footbridge)
Open	April through mid-October (approximately)
Amenities	Vault toilets, potable water (available in North Pines Campground)
Reservation	Walk-in only

Tuolumne Meadows Backpackers' Campground	
Location	Inside the Tuolumne Meadows Campground, behind loop A
Open	July through late September (approximately)
Amenities	Flush toilets, potable water (available in Tuolumne Meadows Campground)
Reservation	Walk-in only

Table 15 – Yosemite Backpackers' Campground Details

Figure 13 – Yosemite Valley and Tuolumne Meadows Campgrounds

High Sierra Camps offer a more "luxurious" wilderness camping experience by providing cozy tent cabins, hot showers, and hearty meals at a nightly rate of $160. The camps are open seasonally and require a reservation. To accommodate the large number of backpackers, park service crews have cleared additional spaces near every High Sierra Camp to serve as basic camping areas with access to the camp's water tap and vault toilet.

Sunrise High Sierra Camp	
Location	~1.5 miles southeast of Sunrise Lakes
Open	July through mid-September (approximately)
Amenities	Restrooms with showers (subject to water availability)
Reservation	http://www.travelyosemite.com/lodging/high-sierra-camps/

Table 16 – Sunrise High Sierra Camp Details

ⓘ Even if you decide to just stay in the basic camping area, you can make advance reservations for breakfast and dinner at the High Sierra Camps. This meals-only option requires a valid wilderness permit and is limited to six reservations per camp.

Whitney Portal (Southern Terminus)

The Whitney Portal Campground has 25 campsites that can be reserved in advance at a nightly rate of $22. Each site features a picnic table, fire ring, and bear box. There are additional first-come, first-served tent campsites in the neighboring Mt. Whitney Trailhead Camp. However, these have a one-night stay limit and are intended for hikers setting out into the wilderness the following day. Showers are available for a $6 fee at the nearby Whitney Portal Store, which also offers hearty meals, cold beverages, smaller backpacking items, and souvenirs. As an alternative to camping, you can book other accommodations in the town of Lone Pine, which you will need to pass through on your way to or from Whitney Portal.

Whitney Portal Campground	
Location	Near the Whitney Portal trailhead parking lot
Open	Mid-May through late October (approximately)
Amenities	Vault toilets, potable water, food storage locker
Reservation	http://www.recreation.gov (search for "Whitney Portal")

Table 17 – Whitney Portal Campground Details

ⓘ Due to the enormous popularity of Yosemite National Park and Mt. Whitney, campsites and other accommodation options usually sell out far in advance, so it is best to book as early as possible.

Along The Route

During your journey from Yosemite National Park to Whitney Portal (or vice versa), you will pass by a number of other established campgrounds and lodging options. Some of these either represent resupply stations or are conveniently located close to them. If you schedule allows, these might be good locations to take a zero day and relax for a bit. With the exception of the Devils Postpile campground, they all require advance reservation. Give them a call to inquire about individual quotes.

Red's Meadow Resort

Red's Meadow Resort (RMR) offers private motel rooms at a nightly rate of $100 and two JMT/PCT hiker cabins, each featuring a set of bunk beds, for $50/night (single person) or $80/night (party of two). Both options include free showers. At the General Store, hikers can pick up their resupply packages, stock up on food, or enjoy a cold beer. The adjacent Mule House Café offers hearty meals and tasty milkshakes.

Red's Meadow Resort	
Location	Near Devils Postpile National Monument
Open	Mid-June through late September (approximately)
Amenities	Bathrooms with shower
Reservation	http://www.redsmeadow.com/resort/resort-lodging/

Table 18 – Red's Meadow Resort Details

For hikers looking to spend a little less, there are two first-come, first-served campgrounds in close proximity to RMR: Devils Postpile Campground (20 sites, $20/night), located near the monument, and Red's Meadow Campground (52 sites, $22/night), located just a short distance up the road from RMR. Both options offer flush toilets, potable water, and bear boxes. Hot showers are available at RMR's shower house for a $7 fee.

Figure 14 – Red's Meadow Store, Café, and Campground

Vermillion Valley Resort

Vermillion Valley Resort (VVR) provides an array of accommodation options, ranging from tent cabins, to a comfortable Yurt, to a motel room complete with shower and kitchenette, to trailers with full kitchens and bathrooms. Nightly rates range from $65 to $107, depending on season and type of accommodation. Additional services include restaurant, grocery store (with limited backpacking supplies), high-speed internet, charging stations (free), hot showers ($6/person), laundry ($6/load), and resupply package handling/storage.

Vermillion Valley Resort	
Location	Western shore of Lake Edison
Open	June through mid-October (approximately)
Amenities	Shower, laundry, picnic table, fire pit, bear box
Reservation	http://www.edisonlake.com/the-resort/accomodations

Table 19 – Vermillion Valley Resort Details

ⓘ As a special bonus to their resupply package service, VVR offers a free beer to JMT/PCT hikers as well as two free nights in a separate tent camping area that is reserved for thru-hikers.

Figure 15 – Vermillion Valley Resort Ferry and Camping Area

Muir Trail Ranch

Muir Trail Ranch (MTR) is a wilderness ranch, located at the halfway mark of the JMT. Backpackers can take advantage of the so-called 'Short Stay' option, which includes a night in a tent cabin ($165/night, shared outhouse) or two nights minimum in a log cabin ($185/night, private bathroom), use of the enclosed hot spring baths, a hearty dinner and breakfast, and a sack lunch for the trail. MTR has a small store stocked with some essentials, like batteries, matches, etc. They will also receive and hold your resupply packages, even if you don't plan to stay there. However, all other services, including meals, hot spring baths/showers, restrooms, and laundry are reserved exclusively for overnight guests.

Muir Trail Ranch	
Location	JMT halfway mark
Open	June through mid-September (approximately)
Amenities	Hot spring, shower, laundry, BBQ
Reservation	http://www.muirtrailranch.com/rates-short.html

Table 20 – Muir Trail Ranch Details

5. Planning & Preparation

Given the challenging profile and remote location of the trail, proper planning and preparation will be key to successfully completing and enjoying the JMT. This can be done in manageable stages, using the guidance provided in this chapter. Ultimately, you'll be able to confidently plunge into this great outdoor adventure knowing everything is properly taken care of.

a. Itinerary

The process of planning your itinerary can be broken down into two stages. The first stage includes all activities concerning long lead items, such as permits and travel arrangements. The resulting 'macro-plan' is the organizational frame of the hiking trip. The second stage focuses on determining the specifics of your hike, such as daily distances and potential campsites. The resulting 'micro-plan' is your personal hiking strategy.

Macro-Planning

The below flow chart outlines the important steps in planning the logistics of your trip. The order shown was determined based on pragmatic considerations and may be altered depending on personal preferences. Individual steps may also be omitted if not applicable.

Figure 16 – Macro-Planning Flow Chart

The most important part of planning your trek on the JMT is securing a permit. This is a time-sensitive task as you must apply 168 days in advance for Yosemite or between February 1 and March 15 for Whitney Portal in order to participate in their respective permit lotteries. Missing the advance reservation windows will significantly decrease your chances of getting the entry trailhead and date you initially wanted. However, you might still be able to reserve a permit at a later point due to cancellations, so be sure to check for permit availability online. As a last resort, you can try to obtain a walk-up permit on-site or alter your itinerary to start from one of the less popular trailheads (as described in Section 4a *Permits*).

In order to prepare your permit request, you will need to decide on your preferred entry point and date, your group size, and your approximate itinerary (incl. exit point and date). Start by estimating your trail days and be realistic about what you can achieve in terms of daily mileage, taking into account your level of fitness and hiking experience. The resulting duration of your hike will impact all of the subsequent macro-planning decisions. Once you know how long it will take you to hike the JMT, check your calendar for times that you would be able to go. Cross-reference your schedule with those of any hiking buddies and make a list of all the date ranges that will work for your group.

Once you have this list, fill out the permit application form required for your chosen entry point and submit it along with your payment for any mandatory fees as soon as the reservation window opens. It may take several attempts and even require flexibility in terms of entry points and dates, but once you have your permit confirmation in hand and the dates locked in, you'll be ready to start booking travel and making all other necessary arrangements for your trip.

Upon completion of the macro-planning stage, you will have the following:

- Rough hiking schedule (starting and ending date)
- Necessary permit reserved (entry and exit point)
- Transportation plan to the entry trailhead
- Transportation plan from the exit trailhead
- Accommodations before and after your hike (if needed)

Micro-Planning

Once your starting and ending dates are set, you will need to breakdown your time on the trail into segments that will dictate your daily mileages and campsite locations as well as your resupply strategy. Your trip legs should be planned around not only the linear distance you expect to travel but also the elevation profile of a particular trail segment. You can expect to take longer to complete sections with significant elevation gain or loss.

The first step is to determine how far you will be able to travel each day. You can either estimate the distance based on your experience from previous hiking trips or calculate your average daily mileage as outlined in Section 2b *Time*. Continuing the example from that section, let's assume your estimate of trail days (ETD) is 17, resulting in an average daily mileage of 13. Using the elevation profiles provided in Appendix B, you can now look at potential campsites that fall within this range, while taking into consideration the difficulty of the respective trail section. Furthermore, make sure you choose campsites that are neither located on a steep incline or decline, nor on a peak or in a basin.

As a second step, consult a topographic map to get a better idea of the surrounding area, access to water, and proximity to special amenities, such as hot springs. Shift your initial target by a mile or two if it is located in difficult or unsuitable terrain, then mark the location on the elevation profile. However, make sure this does not lead to any daily sections that exceed your estimated average by more than 20%, unless the terrain is particularly flat or features a gentle downhill. Repeat this process for each day of your trip until you have a viable plan.

Don't forget to incorporate you resupply stops in your itinerary. A typical bear canister can hold between six and ten days' worth of food, depending on your calorie requirements and packing skills. Consequently, with an ETD of 17, you might be able to get away with only one resupply stop, whereas a more relaxed schedule will likely require two or more resupplies.

Figure 17 below exemplifies the iterative campsite planning process, using a sample elevation profile from Appendix B.

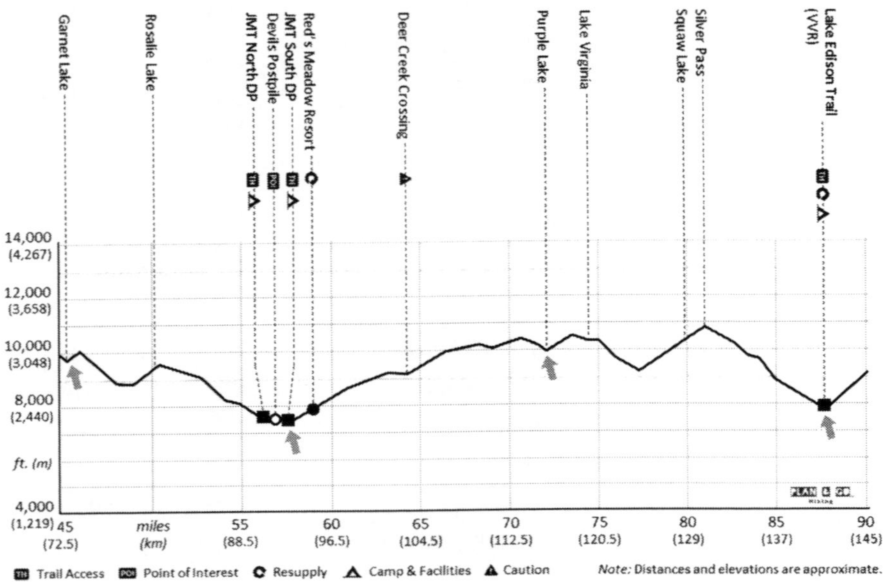

Figure 17 – Micro-Planning Sample Elevation Profile

The campsite and resupply locations you've highlighted in your elevation profile can then be transferred to the topographic map you'll most likely be using to navigate along the trail. Of course, you may decide to alter your itinerary as you progress on your hike, but having the initial trail sections marked on your map will provide a good reference for staying on track with your overall schedule.

! Use caution when planning any side trips and be sure to factor in the additional mileage as it will not appear on the elevation profile.

b. Food

During your 221-mile journey, you will be dependent on your own food rations for the most part, since there is only a handful of options for dining and replenishing snacks. However, having an adequate amount of food is essential for restoring energy levels and keeping spirits up. Looking forward to a good meal on the trail is motivational and having a satisfied stomach lets you fall asleep more contentedly at night. Putting effort into planning and preparing balanced meals with a lot of variety is well worth it. There is nothing worse than eating a meal that brings you little or no enjoyment. Refer to Appendix G for a comprehensive list of food suggestions.

Below are some guidelines for choosing the right kind of food when planning your trail menu:

- Nutritional value: choose high energy foods and ensure an adequate supply of vitamins and minerals
- Calorie distribution: balance approximately 15% protein, 60% carbohydrates, and 25% fat per meal
- Non-perishable: your food must not spoil for a week or longer at up to 90°F (30°C)
- Weight: your food should be as dry and light as possible (including packaging)
- Ease of preparation: save gas, time, dirty pots, and nerves after a long day of hiking

Two factors are particularly important to consider when determining how much food to bring on your journey – calorie value and pack space. Your meals should provide approximately 1.5-2 times the calories you usually consume per day. Calculate higher calories when in low temperatures and vice versa. Additional hunger can be satisfied with snacks. As with any multi-day backpacking trip, pack space is always at a premium. Make sure all food items have a dense nutritional value and are worth their weight and space. The less space you have, the less water and air content should be in your food packaging.

As a rule of thumb, aim for about 1-2 pounds (½-1kg) of food per person per day.

While out on the trail, all of your food and scented items must be stored in an approved bear-resistant container. Although some of the camping areas provide food lockers, this is not a viable option to cover the entire distance. Consequently, you will be required to carry your own bear canister. In addition to keeping your food safe from all the furry animals that will want a taste, the bear canister will also limit the total volume of food you can take with you, since it can only fit so much. Bear canisters come in a variety of styles and sizes, which are further discussed in Section 6d *Food & Water*.

In order to avoid space issues, it helps to repackage your food into single servings, let out any air, and cut off excess packaging. Zip lock bags work well as they can be labeled and reused for packing out waste. As you pack your food in your bear canister, try to make layers of meals per day rather than packing all breakfasts at the bottom, and so forth. This makes accessing your food more convenient. Furthermore, pack the most perishable food items at the top of your canister for early consumption.

In addition to your main meals, well-chosen snacks and supplements can provide valuable nourishment as well. As temperatures rise, it is vital to replenish electrolytes, such as sodium, chloride, potassium, magnesium, manganese, and calcium, on a consistent basis. High water intake without electrolyte replacement over many hours can lead to *hyponatremia*, a life-threatening condition where your body does not have enough salts to function. Adding salty snacks (pretzels, goldfish, salted nuts, or chips) and/or supplements to your trail diet helps avoid electrolyte imbalance.

! If you are on a low sodium diet, ask your doctor if a higher sodium intake while on the trail would be appropriate for you.

As you plan your meals, mind the respective cooking times and utensils needed for preparation. Anything that requires boiling for over ten minutes can be bothersome and can consume too much fuel. Similarly, excessive in-camp preparations, such as cutting, peeling, and mashing, or meals that require a lot of attention can be a hassle when exhausted or overly hungry. Many hikers plan their meals so that the only cooking gear required is a small gas stove, one pot, and one spoon. Nevertheless, whatever meals you decide to go with, bring along adequate equipment and know your own patience.

Despite the above suggestions, some people might choose not to prepare any meals at all. During our JMT trip, we met a 64-year-old hiker who ate nothing but power bars. He said he was quite content and did not get sick of them over the course of his 15(!) trail days. Others may choose to eat a quick cereal bar for breakfast, warm up while packing up, and get going faster to save time and gas needed for a hot breakfast later. You may also decide to alternate your food strategy depending on the campsite you are staying at, the arrival time, and the difficulty of the day ahead. For example, scenic spots and shorter trail days may invite you to enjoy a relaxing morning coffee or spend a long evening with celebratory dining. Ultimately, your food strategy is a matter of your personal preference, your overall itinerary, access to food and gas, and your resupply strategy.

c. Resupply

All but extreme hikers will need at least one resupply on the JMT. Typically, bear canisters can hold 6-10 days' worth of food, depending on how much food you budget and how well you package, compress, and pack it. So, if your itinerary exceeds the restrictions of the bear canister, then sending yourself food and goods to a pick-up location is a simple solution.

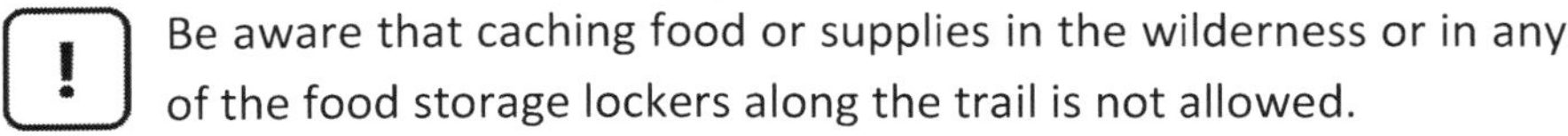
Be aware that caching food or supplies in the wilderness or in any of the food storage lockers along the trail is not allowed.

There are three options for your resupply: You can send yourself a package (1) to a resupply cabin, (2) to a nearby post office, or (3) you can arrange for a resupply drop-off close to you. Post offices are the cheapest option, but they are far off the trail and have limited office hours. Scheduled drop-offs are extremely convenient, but they are also the most expensive and inflexible option. Resupply cabins have the advantage that they often sell other food and hiking gear items (especially stove gas, which cannot be mailed). They sometimes also offer additional amenities, like a restaurant or showers. Some cabins have cache bins where hikers drop excess food, swap, or stock up on things. There, you can usually find essentials, like rice, cereal, and nuts, but also sunscreen and other goods. However, do not rely on using these cache bins and be considerate of the Pacific Crest Trail hikers traveling 2,665 miles (4,288km) from Mexico to Canada, who may depend on the left-behind goodies.

Packing Your Resupply

As packaging for your resupply, choose a watertight and rodent-resistant container. Do not use standard cardboard boxes, as they may get soaked and/or chewed through by mice while sitting in a remote mountain cabin waiting to be picked up. A proven container is a plastic bucket with lid from the hardware store (usually 5 gallon and around $5). Although the lid seals rather tightly, it should be securely taped down along with the handle. If you intend to use one bucket per person per resupply, keep in mind that bear canisters commonly used on the JMT have a capacity of only around 3 gallons (more on this in Section 6d). The additional space can be used to pack one day's worth of extra food and goodies to be consumed right away.

For this extra ration, you can (and should) go all out. Apples and carrots keep well, and eating something fresh will be one of your strongest cravings. Another treat may be wine (in a carton, as you will not want to carry out a bottle) or other sweets and goodies. The more essential content of your resupply should include the planned meals and snacks for the remainder of your trip (or trip section), toilet paper, sunscreen, vitamin & mineral supplements, blister treatment, bandages, and other things you might have used up by then. It helps to make a pack list of items and/or spread them out on the floor, grouping them in days and "extras" (e.g., sunscreen) to make sure you have everything and in the right quantities (see Appendix G for additional remarks).

Resupply Cabins

Figure 18 below shows the locations of the three resupply cabins typically used by JMT hikers. Depending on your itinerary and the amount of food you plan to carry, you may have to arrange for at least one extra resupply in the southern half of the trail. To do so, you could either hire a pack station to deliver your resupply package or you could exit the JMT via Onion Valley (OV) to take advantage of a lodging & resupply opportunity in Independence. Both options are discussed in more detail further below.

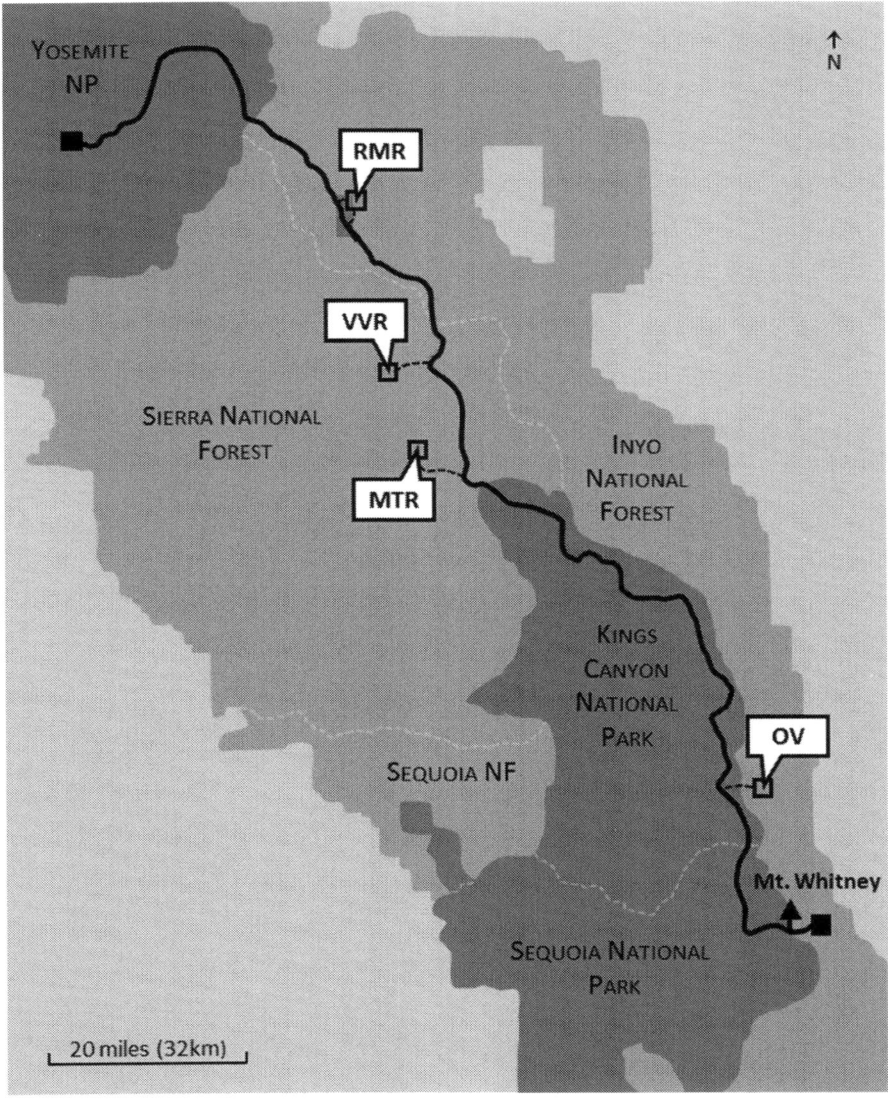

Figure 18 – Overview Map of Resupply Options

Red's Meadow Resort

Red's Meadow Resort (RMR) is located near Devils Postpile, a magnificent rock formation that lies opposite the JMT on the other side of the Middle Fork San Joaquin River. To get to RMR when heading south, leave the JMT for 2.1 miles (3.4km) near Soda Springs and walk right past Devils Postpile. Alternatively, you can stay on the JMT and take the marked RMR junction cut-off.

Location:	59 miles (97km) from Happy Isles, Yosemite
Detour:	Direct access via Devils Postpile and 0.6 mile (1km) round-trip from RMR Junction
Price:	$40/bucket for mail-in, $3/day holding fee for hand-delivered packages
Carriers:	U.S. Postal Service only
Website:	http://www.redsmeadow.com

Red's Meadow Resort			
Stove gas/fuel	Yes	Showers for hikers	Yes
Food and other gear for sale	Yes	Food cache	No
Restaurant for hikers	Yes	Lodging/camping	Yes

Table 21 – RMR Resupply Details

ⓘ There are hot springs and restrooms at the Red's Meadow Campground, 0.6 miles (1km) north of RMR, right off the Reds Cir road. The hot spring is located behind the old abandoned shower house. Soaking in warm water after a few trail days is incredible.

Vermilion Valley Resort

Vermilion Valley Resort (VVR) is located at the western shore of Lake Edison. Southbound hikers leave the JMT at Lake Edison Junction and either take the water taxi after 1.4 miles (2.3km) or continue to hike for 4.8 miles (7.7km) along the north shore of the lake. Northbound hikers exit the JMT at Bear Ridge Junction and walk approximately 7.8 miles (12.6km) along the Bear Ridge Trail, across the dam, and along the shore.

Southbound hikers who don't mind omitting a few miles of the official JMT route can opt to approach VVR via Goodale Pass rather than via Silver Pass. Generally considered a much more pleasant hike, the bypass takes you straight to the resort, skipping the ferry altogether. For more details, refer to the VVR website or search the internet for "Goodale Pass Bypass".

Location: 88 miles (142km) from Happy Isles, Yosemite
Detour: ~8 miles (13km), depending on routes taken
Price: $25/bucket (Jun-Sep), $45/bucket (May/Oct); Water taxi: $12 one-way, $21 round-trip (no reservation needed)
Carriers: UPS (recommended), U.S. Postal Service
Website: http://www.edisonlake.com

Vermilion Valley Resort			
Stove gas/fuel	Yes	Showers for hikers ($6)	Yes
Food and other gear for sale	Yes	Food cache	Yes
Restaurant for hikers	Yes	Lodging/camping	Yes

Table 22 – VVR Resupply Details

The water taxi usually runs from June 1 to October 1, depending on snow and water levels. Additionally, there is a shuttle that will take southbound hikers back to the JMT near Bear Ridge or Bear Creek for $10.

VVR offers two nights in the Hiker Camping area for free. On-site laundry is also available for $6 per load (incl. soap).

Muir Trail Ranch

Muir Trail Ranch (MTR) is located most centrally between Yosemite and Mt. Whitney, along the trail to Florence Lake via which their and your supplies are shipped. Southbound hikers exit the JMT at the North MTR/Sallie Keyes cut-off and descend for approximately 1 mile (1.6km). Northbound hikers leave the JMT at the South MTR cut-off and head towards Blayney Meadows and Florence Lake. MTR has 10+ large cache buckets.

Location: 108 miles (174km) from Happy Isles, Yosemite
Detour: 1 mile (1.6km)
Price: $75/bucket (up to 25 lbs.), $2 per pound in excess
Carriers: U.S. Postal Service (Priority Mail recommended)
Website: http:// www.muirtrailranch.com

Muir Trail Ranch			
Stove gas/fuel	Yes	Showers for hikers	No
Food and other gear for sale	Yes	Food cache	Yes
Restaurant for hikers	No	Lodging/camping	Yes

Table 23 – MTR Resupply Details

ⓘ There is a hot spring amidst high grass and bushes next to a crystal clear lake at the southern end of Shooting Star Meadow, just 0.6 miles (1km) south of MTR, across the San Joaquin River. You should not miss this spot. Enter the coordinates 37.234051, -118.88251 in your GPS device or ask for directions at MTR.

Post Offices

United States Post Offices offer a service called 'General Delivery' which allows you to ship packages to a designated office location, and they will hold it for up to 30 days. There are some scattered post offices in the vicinity of the JMT, but most of them cannot be easily reached. Somewhat accessible is the Mammoth Lakes Post Office approximately 60 miles (96km) from Happy Isles, Yosemite. Getting there requires a detour of approximately 18 miles (29km) round trip from the JMT. Should you decide to send yourself a package for general delivery, be sure to address it as follows:

[First & Last Name]
GENERAL DELIVERY
[Town], [State] [Zip Code]-9999
HOLD UNTIL: [Date]

The zip code extension "-9999" indicates general delivery. For more information on specific post office locations and their business hours, refer to *http://www.usps.com*.

Resupply Delivery

For most JMT hikers, a resupply delivery or 'dunnage drop' is not the most economical form of replenishing food. The deliveries require a packer and one mule per 150 lbs. of load. Packers cost approximately $220 per day, mules cost approximately $100 per day. Some trips require more than one day. It is best to get in touch with the pack stations directly and request a quote based on your specific needs. Below are the two most-cited pack stations:

Rainbow Pack Outfitters

Located on the South Fork of Bishop Creek, serving the John Muir Wilderness and Sequoia and Kings Canyon National Parks. Resupply delivery atop Bishop Pass or down to Le Conte Canyon, approximately 135 miles (217km) from Happy Isles, Yosemite.

Website: http://www.rainbowpackoutfit.com
Phone: +1 (760) 873-8877

Sequoia Kings Pack Train

Located west of Independence, serving the John Muir Wilderness and Sequoia and Kings Canyon National Parks. The Sierra Nevada's oldest continuing pack outfitter. Resupply services, showers, and store.

Website: http://www.sequoiakingspacktrain.com
Phone: +1 (800) 962-0775 (summer), +1 (760) 387-2627 (winter)

For additional information on available pack stations and resupply delivery options see Appendix H.

Lodging & Resupply in Independence (via Onion Valley)

Another viable option for hikers wanting to resupply in the southern half of the trail is to exit the JMT via the Kearsarge Pass Trail, approximately 180 miles (290 km) from Happy Isles, and spend a night in the town of Independence. The *Mt. Williamson Motel and Base Camp* offers an attractive deal to all JMT and PCT hikers if they book a night in one of their fully-equipped cabins or rooms ($85-$125/night, rates vary by season). As part of the package, the motel staff will hold any resupply package you send in advance, they will pick you up and drop you off at the Onion Valley trailhead, and you'll enjoy a hearty breakfast before your departure.

Website: http://www.mtwilliamsonmotel.com
Phone: +1 (760) 878-2121

d. Training

For many hikers, the JMT will be their greatest adventure to date, as well as their greatest mental and physical challenge. Don't be afraid to accept it! With appropriate training, a solid foundation of physical fitness, and the right mindset, you will revel in your accomplishment and soon seek the next one.

Mental Preparation

The right attitude in every phase of a long-distance hike is just as important as proper physical and logistical preparation. From the moment you make the decision, through the weeks of planning your trip, to the final day on the trail, maintaining an open mind and a resilient attitude in coping with obstacles is essential. At any given point, you may be confronted with fatigue, anxiety, or doubt. In those difficult moments, remind yourself why you chose to take on this challenge in the first place and that even the smallest steps in the right direction will help you achieve the goal eventually.

Physical Preparation

Endurance and strength are indispensable assets when it comes to completing the demanding 221 miles of the JMT. If your body is not used to walking long distances on a daily basis while carrying the extra weight of up to 45 lbs. (20kg), it will need proper conditioning. Individual workout needs may vary based on age, health, current fitness level, and other factors. However, the general intention is to get your body moving and comfortable with being active early on, and then gradually increase the intensity.

A good training routine will incorporate cardiovascular exercises and weight lifting elements. Go hiking frequently and participate in other forms of aerobic fitness, like cycling, swimming, running, or group fitness classes. This will not only increase your endurance but also build confidence and momentum for your adventure. In addition, it is advisable to exercise with light to medium weights to strengthen shoulder and back muscles.

A good training exercise is the '90-degree lateral dumbbell raise'. Stand with your feet at shoulders' width, your back slightly slanted forward, and your core muscles engaged. Start by holding the weights in your hands with your elbows at a 90-degree angle touching your ribs and your forearms extended straight in front of your body. In a slow, smooth motion, raise elbows from your ribs to shoulder's height. Hold briefly and return to the starting position.

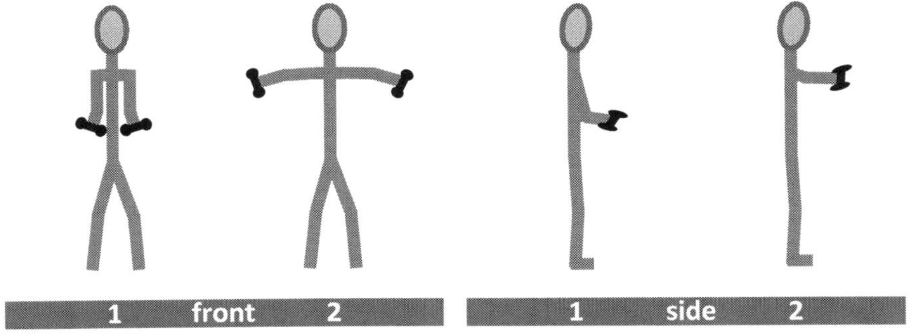

Figure 19 – 90-Degree Dumbbell Lateral Raise

Choose a weight that allows you to do at least three sets of 15-20 repetitions and remember to engage both your abdominal as well as your lower back muscles to support a sturdy stance.

As your fitness level develops, it is crucial to add weight to some of your cardio exercises to simulate the backpack you will be carrying on the trail. Begin by wearing an empty pack, then a partially weighted pack, and eventually the equivalent weight of what you plan to carry during the trip. For an even better training effect, gradually progress your practice hikes to steeper terrain.

The areas of your body most heavily stressed during the hike are your feet, shins, knees, back, and hips. If you've had problems with any of these parts historically, it will be particularly important to do some long training hikes to gauge and prepare for how your body will respond to the conditions on the JMT.

Hiking Style

It is important to adopt a good hiking style in order to use your energy efficiently and keep strains to your joints and tendons to a minimum. This includes hiking at a sustainable pace, taking small controlled steps, and placing your feet in the direction of the slope.

Hike at a Sustainable Pace

The JMT is an ultra-ultra marathon, not a sprint. From an athletic point of view, this means that you need to keep your metabolism and energy conversion in an aerobic state. In brief, aerobic metabolism means that your muscles are receiving enough oxygen from your lungs, sufficient fuel through your bloodstream, and have enough time to dispose of by-products from burning the fuel, especially lactic acid.

The aerobic state or respiration is usually the sweet spot for your body to process its energy, from a nutritional intake as well as fat storage perspective. Keep in mind that even very fit people have an average body fat level of 5-15 percent. That means that a 160-lbs. (75kg) person would have around 16 lbs. (7kg) of fat which contain approx. 56,000 calories – enough caloric energy for over 20 days. This body fat is a valuable reserve you should tap on the trail in order to keep your packed food weight low and potentially reduce your body weight as a pleasant side effect. Maintaining a sustainable pace will allow you to do just that.

Your personal sustainable pace will vary depending on your level of fitness, the elevation, trail conditions, and even the temperature, among other factors. Finding your personal sustainable pace is simple. It is the pace at which you breathe deeply, but not rushed, you may sweat, but never excessively, you feel you could hike like this for hours without having to stop for extended breaks frequently. As a result, a slow but sustainable pace will be the fastest way, because you will feel less fatigue and need less rest/recovery time.

Take Small Steps

In line with maintaining a sustainable pace, small steps avoid stress peaks for your muscles, reduce the force of impact on your joints, and minimize the likelihood of an injury due to misstep. You will be climbing and descending a number of tall rock or dirt steps as well as sparsely-marked landslide fields along the trail. Instead of leaping or taking a large step, you can use 2-3 well-placed steps to reduce the effort you would need to expend on a single ambitious move. Taking small, conscious steps keeps the strain to your muscles to a minimum, avoiding muscle ache.

Especially when hiking uphill with a full pack, small steps will reduce exhaustion and extend your range. Likewise, descending with a full pack causes many to suffer from knee and ankle pain. The larger the step, the greater the vertical drop and, hence, the greater the impact to your joints. Lastly, small steps are less likely to go wrong. A small step has less momentum that could potentially cause you to twist your ankle or slip on loose gravel. Since emergency access to the JMT is limited, avoiding any injury is the best way to go.

Always Place Your Feet in the Direction of the Slope

The last recommendation is especially important when hiking downhill. Look at the direction and angle of the slope. Always place your foot so that it is in-line with the direction of the slope of the trail. If the path is going straight down the mountain, your toes should also point straight down. If there are switchbacks, you should adhere to the respective slope of the trail.

Why? Think of it this way: If you do slip, you want your toes to shoot forward so that you fall backwards. You may land on your bottom or your backpack, but both are padded. If you had your foot sideways and slipped, your body weight would follow the slope and push forward, twisting your ankle and potentially causing a painful injury at an inconvenient location.

Trekking Poles

Trekking poles offer some definite advantages on a multi-day backpacking trip. They may extend your daily distance by up to 25%, because they increase the efficiency of each step and help conserve energy. They also keep your hands up and help with circulation in the arms, preventing your fingers from swelling. When carrying a heavy pack, especially one in which the weight is not evenly distributed, you can easily lose your balance. Using trekking poles guarantees three points of contact on the ground at all times and, thus, increases your stability.

On the JMT, you will also cross a number of rivers and streams, some on narrow logs, others on stepping-stones. Your poles are especially handy here when a misstep can leave you with wet feet or worse! You may even have to ford a river if water levels are high, so you will certainly want trekking poles to maintain your stability, especially when you cannot see where you are stepping. When descending, trekking poles can be used to slow down your forward movement and take the stress off of your knees. However, make sure to not overly strain your shoulders while relieving your knees.

Make sure your poles are adjusted to a comfortable height, so that on a flat surface you are neither leaning too far forward or have your elbows bent at over 90 degrees. If you know you will be descending a steep section of trail for a prolonged period, you may want to lengthen the poles to prevent you from leaning too far forward. Conversely, you may wish to shorten the poles on prolonged steep uphill sections to help with the climb.

ⓘ If you're new to using hiking poles, it would be wise to familiarize yourself with the right technique, for which you will find plenty of video tutorials on the internet. Try them out on a few training hikes to see how they feel and to get in a bit of practice before you hit the trail.

* * *

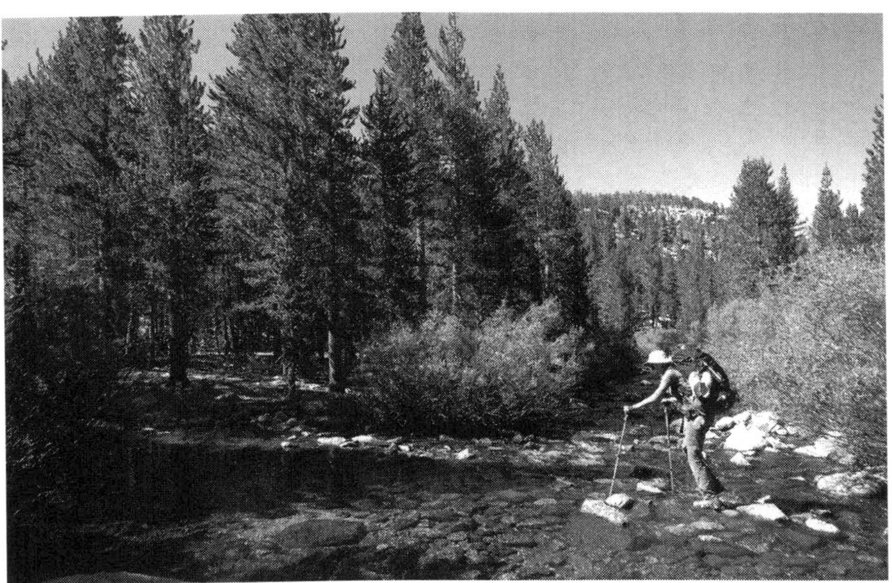

Figure 20 – Using Trekking Poles to cross Wallace Creek

6. Gear

Choosing the right gear for any multi-day backpacking trip is an essential component to creating a memorable and enjoyable experience. However, gear selection could easily be a separate book in itself. The following overview is intended to introduce the most commonly used items and provide JMT-specific recommendations. To find the items that work best for you, it's a good idea to consult additional sources, like online product descriptions and customer reviews, talk to experts at outdoor gear stores, and ultimately put everything to the test before your trip.

a. Clothing

"My face is sweating, but I'm still freezing." – This is a normal morning in the High Sierra. While the clear air and high altitudes allow the sun to shine vigorously even during early hours, they also make for rapid temperature drops after sunset. So if you are hiking during the summer months, apart from the occasional rain shower, days will be warm and nights will be cold. It's that simple.

Recap: Layering

Layering your clothing will maximize your comfort on the trail. It is a simple, proven concept that allows you to make quick adjustments based on your activity level and changes in weather/temperature. The first layer against your skin is called the *base layer*. It includes your underwear and hiking shirts. The base layer helps control your body temperature by moving perspiration away from your skin, so fabrics with excellent moisture-wicking capabilities are highly preferable. The next layer, called *middle layer*, provides insulation to help retain heat by trapping air close to your body. This could be a fleece jacket or puffy down jacket. The outer layer, called the *shell layer*, provides protection from the elements. A lightweight windbreaker that is somewhat water-resistant will be a good choice in conditions where cold drafts are more likely than heavy rain.

Remember to avoid any kind of clothing that is made of cotton, as it rapidly absorbs moisture, takes a long time to dry, and loses its ability to keep you warm when it gets wet. Clothing specifically designed for hiking and made from various synthetic materials or wool (e.g., merino wool) is a much better choice for any long-distance hike.

Warm – 9:00 AM to 6:00 PM

During the day, most hikers wear shorts or light hiking pants. Pants keep dust off your legs, which is a bit of an issue on the dry trails, and provide sun protection. Shorts are cooler and generally less restrictive. On this note, make sure your underwear does not rub and chafe your thighs, even when moist. Biker shorts without padding can be a good option.

A (short sleeve) T-shirt is sufficient temperature-wise while you are in motion, but long-sleeved and high-collared shirts offer lotion-free sun protection. There are light, classic-cut button shirts with folding collars as well as thin, long-sleeved T-shirts with high zipper collars.

If possible, pick a shirt without seams on the shoulders to avoid rubbing and pressure points from your pack straps.

Most hikers also opt for some form of headwear – a wide-brimmed hat, visor, base cap, cap with neck flap, or other. Given the expectable heat, any option should be well-vented and provide good UV protection. Southbound hikers will get more sun in their face, while northbound hikers receive more rays on their neck.

Cold – 6:00 PM to 9:00 AM

As the sun disappears behind the surrounding peaks, you will quickly miss your midday nemesis. A good first warming layer is a light merino wool sweater or fleece jacket. When you have settled at camp, sitting and waiting for dinner, you will want to add another layer. Puffy down jackets offer great warmth for their weight and compress well. Puffy synthetic jackets are a cost effective alternative. And to be fully-prepared, you should also bring one light outer shell rain jacket or windbreaker.

If you decided to walk in shorts during the day, it is still advisable to bring a pair of pants or long johns for the evenings. Then, in your sleeping bag, long underwear bottoms and long sleeve tops are best suited to keep your sleeping bag clean and yourself warm. If you choose comfortable long sleeve T-shirts for hiking, a clean one works well for sleeping, too. Useful accessories for the cold are a fleece or knitted beanie and/or a multi-functional scarf to keep your head warm at camp. Gloves for packing up and holding your trekking poles in the morning are very nice to have.

Additional Tips

Consider bringing a pair of flip-flops, sandals, or other light footwear to wear at camp. Knowing you can take your shoes off after a long day of hiking becomes ever more appealing with every mile traveled. Choose a lightweight, water-repellent (or, at least, quick-drying) option that could also be worn for fording rivers.

As for washing your clothes, items with less pockets and zippers will dry faster and are less likely to damage one another during the process. Since water is abundant and the air is dry, you can rinse your clothing pretty much every day and it will dry fast, allowing you to pack less items overall.

[!] To avoid contamination of natural water sources, wash your clothes at least 200 feet (60m) away from any stream or lake. Plastic bear canisters make excellent laundry drums. Refrain from using any type of detergent or, at least, opt for bio-degradable options.

Sample Clothing List

This was my clothing pack list:

2 pairs of hiking socks
2 pairs of underwear
1 pair of long underwear
1 pair of shorts
1 pair of hiking pants
1 long sleeve T-shirt (with zip collar)
1 T-shirt
1 fleece jacket
1 warm (!) puffy jacket
1 rain shell
1 visor
1 beanie

b. Hiking

Standard hiking gear consists of appropriate footwear, additional ankle and leg protection, a fitting and well-balanced backpack, and optional trekking poles. This section provides an overview of available options and features, discusses pros and cons, and offers advice on JMT-specific items.

Footwear

"Hiking shoes or trail runners?" This is one of the most frequently asked questions in JMT-related online groups and forums. In fact, it is a highly controversial subject discussed throughout the entire long-distance hiking community. Unsurprisingly, the answer to the question is not trivial, since there are many individual and trail-specific factors that need to be taken into consideration. It is safe state, however, that your footwear will be the most stressed piece of gear on your trip. Key features to look for (regardless of type or model) include a thick, cushioned sole with non-slip tread, sufficient support for you and the weight you are carrying, and self-evidently a perfect fit. Beyond that, personal preferences may differ regarding stability, comfort, breathability, and weight.

Hiking Boot	Hiking Shoe	Trail Runner

Figure 21 – Hiking Footwear Options

Hiking Boots

Hiking Boots provide the most stability overall. A well-fitting boot is snug, supports the ankle, and reduces the risk of twisting on a slight misstep. With more contact area, the foot is less likely to move back and forth in a good boot. The high-rising sides also offer ankle protection from hitting rocks and prevent sand and dust from entering the boot. Other advantages are warmth and water resistance, which may be desirable during the JMT shoulder season, when snowpack is still present. Drawbacks of boots are the greater weight, stiffness, and lower breathability.

Hiking Shoes

Hiking Shoes combine the grip stability of a good boot with more flexibility. The low cut allows more mobility and light mesh uppers enable moisture wicking. Look for a pair with firm heel support and a plastic or rubber tip to protect your toes. Different brands have different lacing systems, some enable great fit in minimal time. Hiking shoes are lighter than boots and generally feel less restrictive while still providing sufficiently firm stability. Drawbacks are potentially more rocks and sand in your shoes, reduced ankle support, and reduced ankle protection.

Trail Runners

Originally designed for longer runs in the mountains or woods, trail runners have become increasingly popular among long-distance hikers as part of the general ultralight backpacking movement. Trail runners combine the agility and low weight of conventional running shoes with the support and grip needed to travel in rough and uneven terrain. Breathable mesh uppers help keep feet cooler on a hot day but will allow particles of sand and dirt to get inside the shoe. The lower weight and less restrictive fit of trail runners make walking in them less exhausting, allowing hikers to extend their daily range. However, in order to save weight, they usually provide less cushioning and protection than hiking shoes or boots. When considering trail runners for the JMT, keep in mind that they are not designed for long hiking trips with heavy backpacks, so your overall gear strategy should reflect your ambition to go ultralight.

In summary, whichever shoe or boot you decide to go with, make sure you are confident about your choice. It should provide adequate support for you and your pack weight, wick moisture away from your feet, not be too heavy and tiring, have a well-cushioned sole, and most importantly a padded inside that does not cause blisters. Furthermore, it is strongly recommended to use your new shoes on a few training hikes to break them in and to see how they feel overall. If in doubt, try another pair – getting your shoes right is essential. Also, refrain from wearing shoes that are too worn down and only have little tread left as it will increase the chances of slipping and falling.

ⓘ Buy your hiking footwear at least half a size bigger than you normally would. This will allow you to wear padded socks for additional comfort and prevent your toes from brushing against the front of the shoe when hiking downhill.

Socks & Gaiters

A good sock can significantly add to your hiking comfort. Most modern trail socks are made of merino wool or polyester. Both fibers have outstanding properties regarding moisture wicking and temperature regulation. Thick socks, especially those with hidden seams, provide cushioning and help the shoe embrace your foot evenly, reducing rubbing and blisters. Although less stylish in a shoes-shorts-combo and slightly warmer, socks that go (well) above your ankle collect less sand and stones, keep your legs cleaner, and provide better protection from the sun and pointy shrubs.

Gaiters can provide even greater protection for your feet and lower legs. They wrap around your ankles and calves and cover the gap between socks and footwear. There are different types of gaiters to choose from depending on the nature of the trip and the conditions expected. Low-rise trail gaiters are perfect for the JMT. They are lightweight, breathable, and provide basic protection against rocks, grit, and snow.

Compression socks can assist circulation and provide additional benefits to those who have issues with blood clots, edema, or thrombosis. They come in different lengths, from knee- and thigh-high to full pantyhose style, and in a variety of compression gradients. Lower gradients are usually prescription-free while higher gradients may require consultation. If you are over 40 years old or have a condition where they could be helpful, it may be wise to get your doctor's opinion on using compression socks during your trek.

Backpacks

Just like shoes, an ill-fitting backpack can be the source of considerable discomfort and even pain. Chafing along straps, restrictive harnesses, poorly adjusted hip belts, and other issues can quickly impact both your speed and enjoyment on the trail.

Choosing a Pack

If this is your first long-distance backpacking trip or you are looking to upgrade to a lighter weight (possibly ultralight) model, below are some tips to help you find a pack that is right for you and the 221-mile challenge at hand. In addition to this information, consider reading online product reviews of various makes and models to see how other hikers have rated a particular pack's performance. Once you've made your decision, take the fully loaded backpack on training hikes before the JMT to make sure it still feels good after long hikes with substantial weight.

Criteria	Comment
Size	Given the wide variety of sizes and styles, it's advisable to get fitted for your pack by a professional at a reputable outdoor outfitter. If you prefer to purchase online, be sure to research how to accurately measure your torso length to avoid ordering a wrong size. To better fit different torso shapes, the design and cut of packs and shoulder straps vary to make them more comfortable for broad- or narrow-shouldered people. Try and compare different packs.
Capacity	Packing capacity is measured in liters. Typical packs used on the JMT have capacities of 60-70 liters. While you want to choose the smallest capacity to save weight, you also need to be able to fit all of your gear.

	The right capacity for you depends on the spatial requirements of your bulkiest items (tent, bear canister, sleeping bag, and pad) and the amount of clothing you plan to bring. If you prefer to fit all your gear inside the pack, opt for a larger capacity. Some models offer more flexibility by allowing you to raise the top lid. If you are ok with strapping larger items (e.g., tent, foam pad) to the outside of your pack, you could choose a smaller capacity. However, this may mean that weight isn't optimally distributed. See the *Packing & Adjusting Your Pack* sections further below for additional information.
Weight	The weight of a pack is directly linked to its capacity, the padding it provides, and the quality of materials used. Thick padding along shoulder straps and hip belts offers additional comfort but also adds weight. Extra durable shell materials protect your gear better and are less prone to tears and punctures but are generally heavier. Ultralight backpacks usually provide less padding and have a thinner shell, requiring more careful handling, especially in the rugged parts of the JMT. Ultralight materials are also more expensive.
Padding	The padding of shoulder straps, hip belt, and where the frame touches your back are essential to how comfortable your pack will be, especially when filled with up to 45 lbs. (20kg) of gear. Using an ultralight backpack saves extra weight but make sure you are comfortable with the limited padding and that there is no rubbing/chafing when the pack is fully-loaded and you are in normal hiking motion.
Adjustability	Most modern internal frame packs are very similar in terms of adjustability. Shoulder straps and hip belts can be adjusted in length; load lifter straps connect the pack's top to the shoulder straps and keep the weight balanced near your center; sternum straps connect the shoulder straps across the chest to snug the pack's fit and increase stability. Some packs have

	an adjustable suspension system, meaning the entire shoulder harness system can be slid up and down to fit the exact torso length. Compression straps along the sides and front of the pack pull the weight close to your center and keep contents from shifting on difficult trails. Daisy chains, elastic straps, trekking pole loops, and other tool loops allow you to arrange and adjust gear on the outside of the pack.
Compartments	A pack with a well thought-out design can make your life a lot easier on the trail. Most packs come with a plethora of pouches, compartments, straps, and other storage amenities. The right combination of compartments is largely a matter of personal preference. Some hikers may insist on a sleeping bag compartment at the bottom of the pack, others may look for a certain number of side pockets to organize and access the contents of their pack, while still others may want one or two water bottle pockets. A large number of pockets and compartments may, however, conflict with a minimalist, ultralight approach.
Ventilation	Choosing a pack with a well-ventilated back area can be a big plus, especially on the hottest sections of the trail. A dry back and shoulders not only add to your general comfort but make your body less susceptible to chafing. Different brands and models have various approaches for wicking moisture and heat from in-between your back and your pack. Some have air channels between padding, others completely separate the pack from the hiker's back with a tension mesh. Some ventilation methods are more effective and/or comfortable than others. Try them out until you find one that you like.
Hydration	Most standard backpacks feature a separate compartment and loop for suspending a hydration reservoir inside the pack. These packs will have a small opening for the drinking tube and elastic rings or clips on the shoulder straps that allow you to attach the hose for

	convenient access. This feature may be more or less relevant depending on your preferred water storage method, which is further discussed in Section 6d.
Frame	Almost all modern packs have the frame sewn directly into the pack. This increases stability, provides more protection, allows for better adjustability, and leads to a better fit overall. However, internal frame packs are a bit heavier and more expensive than their dated external frame counter-parts. Ultralight models cut down on the pack's supporting structure even further to save weight.
Rain cover	Built-in rain covers are practical but not essential for the JMT given the low chance of rain. If you decide to bring one anyway, you could use it as a protective layer to prevent rodents from chewing through your backpack at night or when left unattended otherwise.

Table 24 – Backpack Selection Criteria

[!] Choosing an ultralight backpack helps reduce overall pack weight, which can lead to less fatigue and an extended daily range. It's important to understand, however, that your overall strategy (and budget) must be aligned, since loading up an ultralight pack with heavy gear is going to make your hike uncomfortable.

Packing your Pack

As you pack your backpack, pay attention to two things: weight distribution and internal organization of your gear. Regarding *weight distribution*, it is important to keep heavy items close to your back and centered both vertically and horizontally (see Figure 22 below). Moderately heavy items should be placed closest to the heavy items, leaving the perimeter of the pack (sleeping bag compartment, exterior straps) for the lightest weight items. The aim is to bring the weight in the backpack as close to the center of your back as possible. This way, the pack's center of gravity is closest to your own, making it less likely for you to lose your balance and reducing the strain on your back.

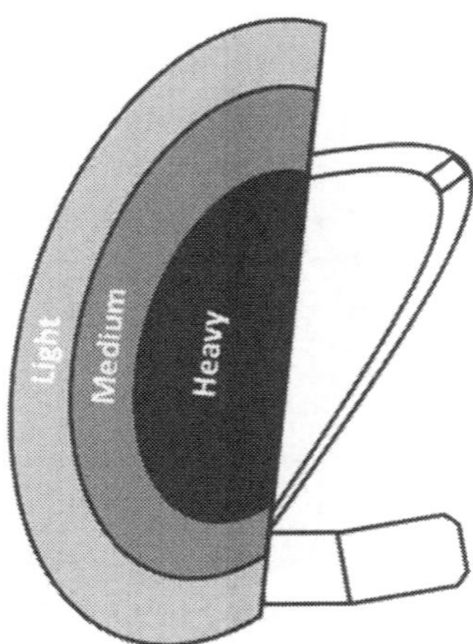

Figure 22 – Ideal Backpack Weight Distribution

A well-planned *internal organization* and distribution of gear among the compartments and pockets of your pack can save time and headaches. Anything that needs easy and frequent access, such as a map, sunscreen, snacks, or a pocket knife, should be stored in an accessible outside pocket or near the top of your pack. Gear that will only be used once at camp can be placed inside and below heavy items. Pack and unpack your gear at home and during your training hikes to determine best packing order and location of various pieces of gear. Sticking to a particular gear organization structure and routine will make it easier to pack your backpack and access crucial gear while on the go.

Using thin plastic bags or (water-resistant) compression sacks can be a good way to further organize your pack's main compartment. You can use these to group certain types of gear (cooking set, sleep clothes, etc.) and make accessing contents more convenient while providing additional protection against water and dirt. Valuables (phone, keys, money) can be kept in a zip lock bag and buried, as they will hardly be needed. Keep rain gear easily accessible, so you can get it out quickly in a thunderstorm. Once you have all your items packed and are ready to hit the trail, pull all the compression straps (usually on the sides and top of your pack) to bring the weight closer to your back and prevent gear from shifting during the hike.

Adjusting your Pack

Step 1: Adjusting your pack starts by putting it on correctly. If your pack is heavy, place one foot forward and lift the pack onto your thigh, a nearby rock or other surface at a convenient level. Then, slip into the shoulder straps and lean forward, pulling the pack onto your back (if you're not familiar with this technique, search for a tutorial video online). As you lean forward, position the pack so the hip belt is centered comfortably over your hip bone, then close and tighten the hip belt firmly.

Step 2: As you straighten yourself up, your shoulder straps should be loose, leaving 100% of the pack's weight on your hips. In this starting position, the shoulder straps should have a gap of approximately one inch over your shoulders. If the straps already put pressure on your shoulders in the starting position and your pack has an adjustable suspension, slide the entire shoulder harness up a little and re-secure it. Now, tighten your shoulder straps until they touch your shoulders.

Step 3: Unlike older backpack designs, today's packs use the hip belt, rather than the shoulder straps, to carry most of the pack weight. Keep this in mind as you adjust and tighten the straps. Pull your load lifters (that extend from the top of your shoulder straps to the top of your pack) to bring the pack's center of gravity closer to yours. Finally, close your sternum strap and tighten comfortably in front of your chest to help reduce the pack's tendency to pull your shoulders back. Once you have everything set, check your shoulder straps one last time to ensure that they are merely guiding the pack weight rather than bearing a lot of it.

Trekking Poles

As outlined in Section 5d *Training*, there are many benefits to hiking with trekking poles. They help you maintain balance in unstable conditions and provide a sense of security on steeper stretches of the trail. Below are some features to look for when purchasing trekking poles:

- Ergonomic grips and comfortable, padded wrist straps. Avoid sweat-prone plastic grips (opt for cork instead) and unpadded straps that will chafe your wrists and hands.
- The length of the pole should be easily adjustable.
- The locking mechanism (twist or external lever) as well as the overall pole should be sturdy.
- The lighter the pole, the better. Lightweight poles will minimize arm fatigue and make them easier to use.
- Shock absorbing springs can be useful but are mostly a matter of taste. Try them out for yourself.
- Rubber tips absorb shock and muffle impact noise. More grip on rock, less on soft subsoil.
- Baskets (plastic discs just above the tip) help give you traction and additional surface area that is useful on sandy soil and snow.

ⓘ If traveling by airplane, be aware that you are not allowed to bring trekking poles as carry-on baggage with you. Be sure to buy trekking poles that can fit inside your backpack or checked luggage. Another option is to attach trekking poles to the outside of your pack and then pack your entire kit inside a protective duffel or heavy-duty trash bag.

c. Sleeping

This section supports your decisions with regards to putting together a comfortable and practical sleeping environment. For most, this will consist of a lightweight tent, sleeping bag, and sleeping pad. However, there are alternatives for those looking to save weight and space in their packs.

Shelters

When choosing a shelter, the decision comes down to how much weight you want to carry, how much money you want to spend, and how much protection you want from the elements. The pros and cons of the four most common shelter options (illustrated in Figure 23) are discussed below. If you are hiking with one or more other people, you might consider sharing a shelter to save weight. However, this should be carefully weighed up against the benefits of having a separate shelter, which will offer a bit of privacy after a long day of hiking together.

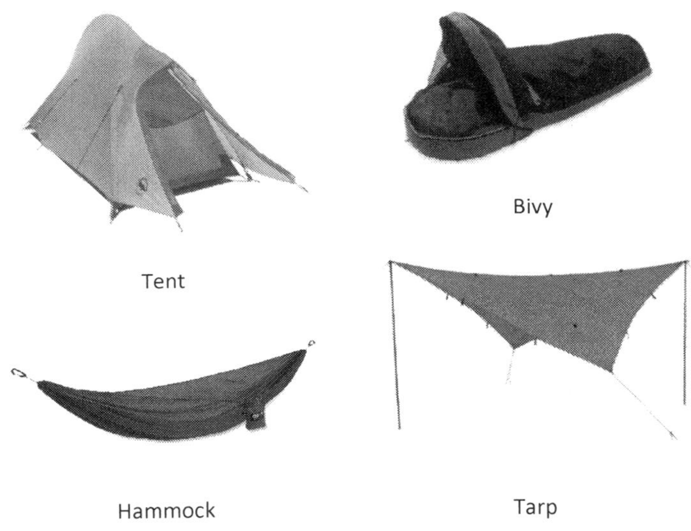

Figure 23 – Sleeping Shelter Options

Tent

The tent is the preferred option of many JMT hikers, as it provides the most space (for hiker and gear) and best protection from the elements, critters, and mosquitoes. While the lightest single person tents are only around 1.5 lbs. (0.7kg), carrying a tent is likely to be the heaviest shelter option. Since most lightweight tents utilize extremely thin fabric, consider taking a footprint to protect the tent floor from punctures and moisture, even though this will add a few ounces. In the event of sustained rain or stormy conditions, pitching a tent and jumping inside will offer instant shelter. Also, retreating into your tent to take a look at the map, while your food is getting ready outside, can be quite cozy on a cold evening. Weather forecast permitting, you could decide to leave the tent's rainfly at home to save on weight. This would also allow for an (almost) unobstructed view of the High Sierra's crystal clear night skies.

ⓘ Tents have more surface area to collect moisture from rain and condensation, which will add weight to your pack. If you don't have time to let it air-dry, consider taking a small viscose sponge to wipe down any moist surface area before packing and hitting the trail.

Bivy

Made of water- and wind-resistant materials, a bivy (short for bivouac sack) is a thin fabric shell that is designed to slip over a sleeping bag to provide additional insulation and protection from the elements (similar to a tent). It has a small hole or breathable fabric in the head area which also features a little dome, giving you some space to breath and rest on your elbows inside. Because the bivy gets in direct contact with the sleeping bag and has less air circulation, inner condensation could become a problem. Unlike tents, bivies offer no additional room for gear or body movement, and people who are uncomfortable in confined spaces may not enjoy the lack of freedom. However, due to their minimalist design, bivies take up much less space in your backpack than a tent and also weigh less. They are also extremely quick to set up and require only little space on the ground. Bivies are ideal for JMT hikers looking for a minimalist shelter that still provides a decent level of protection.

Under the Stars/Tarp

To anyone counting ounces, a tent or even a bivy may seem like unnecessary extra weight. The lightest alternative would be to sleep under the stars in your sleeping bag with the aid of a ground sheet and a tarp in case of rain. However, according to the saying, "it never rains at night in the High Sierra", you have a very good chance of waking up dry. That is, as long as you have been diligent in selecting your campsite. This minimalist approach (also referred to as "cowboy camping") certainly helps to reduce pack weight but lacks the all-around protection and insulation of a tent or a bivy.

Still, it offers a chance to experience nature up close and personal and to fully appreciate the spectacular night sky. When choosing to camp under the stars, make sure your sleeping bag is adequate to combat the expected nighttime temperatures including the wind-chill. Despite the marginal protection and lack of privacy, many minimalist hikers consider cowboy camping a more than viable option for the JMT.

Hammock

In areas with ample trees of sufficient strength, hammocks are a great alternative to 1-person tents. Their structure promises exceptional comfort (depending on your preferred sleeping position) as well as independence from underground surfaces and slopes, offering more flexibility in choosing campsites. When properly set up using wide tree straps, hammock systems have a lower impact on vegetation versus pitching a tent or tarp on forest soil. Hammock campers are more sensitive to cooling from underneath, thus, potentially requiring additional insulation (e.g., down underquilt or foam padding). Basic hammocks with no extras may help save pack weight, however, a complete hammock system, including insulation, rainfly, and mosquito net, can weigh just as much if not more than a standard ground system. Using a hammock on the JMT is doable, but you'll have to be much more strategic about planning your itinerary, since camping will be confined to below the treeline. Setting up at lower elevations may not be as scenic, and mosquitoes can be a real nuisance. In areas where hanging a hammock is simply not possible, like Guitar Lake or Trail Camp, you'll need to be prepared to either cowboy camp or set up a (redundant) ground system.

During my trip, I used a 1-person tent with footprint and was very content with my decision. My sleeping bag/pad combo was not adequate at all (see Section 7a *Plan* for details), so I was grateful for the shelter. As additional insulation, I spread a silver emergency blanket beneath my sleeping pad to block the ground's creeping cold. I appreciated being able to keep my belongings under the vestibule and packing/unpacking in a dirt-free environment inside. I enjoyed an evening routine of moving inside the tent, changing, applying a soothing balm to my ankles and knees, hanging my light inside my tent, reviewing the map and comparing actual to planned distances travelled, taking short diary notes, and finally preparing for the next day.

Sleeping Bags

Sleeping bags come in an overwhelming range of varieties depending on their primary purpose. It is all the more important to understand which features are essential for a multi-day backpacking adventure on the JMT. A sleeping bag is a significant investment that should last for 10+ years if cared for properly. When choosing a model, there are three primary factors to consider: warmth, weight, and pack size.

Warmth

Warmth, expressed by the bag's temperature rating, will probably be the most important criteria in bag selection. Fortunately, there is an EN Standard[4] warmth measurement that lets you easily compare different models. Choose a bag with a temperature rating equal to or lower than the average monthly low temperature for wherever you will be camping. For the JMT, a 3-season bag rated between 20°F and 30°F (-6°C and -1°C) should suffice for most people, but if you tend to be cold or hot when you sleep, be sure to factor that in.

ⓘ For additional warmth, consider a sleeping bag liner (made of silk, cotton, fleece, or synthetic materials) which can add 5-15 degrees to your bag. This will also help keeping your bag clean of dirt and body oils that can degrade its warmth over time.

Peak performance sleeping bags use down insulation with fill-powers[5] of 700-900 or an equivalent synthetic composition. Down is breathable and provides an incredible loft and resulting insolation while being lightweight

---

[4] EN Standard 13537: a European Standard (also used by some U.S. companies) for the testing, rating, and labelling of sleeping bags.

[5] Fill-power: a measure of loft in cubic inches; it describes to what volume one ounce of down expands to.

and compressing well. Additionally, there are new hydrophobic/dry downs that either repel moisture or maintain insulation properties even after getting wet. Modern synthetic fill materials mimic the great properties of down, often at a very competitive price. However, they are generally heavier and don't compress as well as down.

Weight

Weight is a general concern. Besides the filling, the weight is a function of length, girth, cut, fabric, and features of the sleeping bag. Length of the bag is usually a pretty clear decision based on your height. Girth will primarily be determined by your shoulders and belly or hips. Cut refers to the bag's shape. Most backpacking bags available today are mummy style that follows the contours of the body. Some bags are cut straight, providing more space but also more material to carry. Fabrics lining the sleeping bag are usually made of lightweight, synthetic materials. Features that enhance the bag's ability to retain heat include a drawstring hoodie to prevent heat loss from your head, a draft tube that covers the zipper to avoid heat loss on the side, and baffles or shingles that trap the down/synthetic fill in compartments to maintain even heat retention.

In order to reduce weight and bulk, many modern backpacking sleeping bags do not have padding on the side you will be lying on. There are two main reasons for this: First, the bag makers assume that most people will use a sleeping pad, which provides cushioning and insulation. Second, lying on the bag's insulation material compresses it, significantly reducing its effectiveness. Down-fill mummy bags will generally have the best warmth-to-weight ratios.

Pack Size

The amount of pack space a sleeping bag takes up is strongly correlated with its temperature rating, weight, and ultimately cost. Reducing the bag weight usually reduces the pack size, and more expensive bags will typically pack down to a smaller size. Warmer bags with more filling typically do not compress as much and will take up more pack space.

Shelter Compatibility

Lastly, your choice of sleeping bag should match your choice of shelter. If you are sleeping with only a tarp or completely without a shelter, your sleeping bag should be especially warm, wind- and water-resistant. Keep in mind that water-resistant shells are less breathable and require more time for your bag to loft. If you plan to save weight on filling by wearing your jacket to sleep, make sure the sleeping bag provides enough inner space for the jacket's loft.

Sleeping Pads

A sleeping pad should literally support a good night's sleep. The two main criteria are cushioning and insulation. After a long day of trekking on the JMT, you will appreciate some sort of sleeping pad. There are three popular and equally suitable alternatives – air pads, self-inflating pads, and foam pads – each with their own trade-offs.

Air Pads

Similar to the ones used in swimming pools, hiking air pads have a thin, air-tight shell that is inflated through a mouth valve. In order to cut down on weight, they are often semi-rectangular in shape. Air pads are very lightweight, can roll-up very small, and offer exceptional cushioning, especially those with a thickness of two inches (5cm) and up. On the downside, inflating a thick pad may require several minutes of lung power from you, which can feel like a chore at the end of the day. Lightweight models can be noisy due to crackling material. Punctures are also a concern, but this can be repaired in the field with the proper materials.

Foam Pads

Usually made of dense, closed-cell foams, foam pads can either be rolled up or folded like an accordion. They are light, inexpensive, provide great insulation, and are practically indestructible even on rough surfaces. When folded up, they also make convenient seats in camp. On the downside, foam pads are usually not very thick and provide limited cushioning comfort. They also do not compress and must therefore be attached to the exterior of your pack.

Self-inflating Foam Pads

Combining the packability of an air pad with the durability of a foam pad while needing only little additional inflation, thin pads are light and can be compressed well to fit into a small sack. On the downside, they offer limited cushioning, while thicker pads of over two inches are often too heavy for backpackers.

ⓘ Whichever option you choose, make sure it fits the dimensions of your body and you are comfortable sleeping on it. Try it out on the floor at home before setting out on the trail to avoid any unpleasant surprises.

On the JMT, I used an ultralight, minimalist frame air pad, which is designed to cushion only the body parts that touch the ground when lying flat (head, shoulders, butt, calves, feet). It was far too cold and uncomfortable, especially if you prefer to sleep on your side, in which case your hip bone will soon hit the ground. There are other excellent lightweight options out there. I now own a very comfortable air pad that is 2.5 inches (6.3cm) thick and only weighs 12 ounces (350g).

Additional Comfort

Apart from the clothing you wear in your sleeping bag, there are other gear items that can provide additional comfort, such as a pillow, eye mask, ear plugs, and insect repellent. An alternative to packing an inflatable pillow is using your sleeping bag's stuff sack as a casing, stuffing it loosely with clothes, or buying a sleeping bag with a pillow case pocket sewn inside. An eye mask can be helpful for people that are very light sensitive, especially during a bright full moon. If you have trouble sleeping near creeks or streams, you may consider taking ear plugs, but be aware that wearing them will make you less aware of rodents or larger animals in the vicinity. Insect repellent can also come in handy, especially when camping near water, or if you decide to sleep in an open shelter or entirely without.

d. Food & Water

While Section 5b discussed the type of food and drinks to bring and send as resupply, this section focuses on the various gear items needed to store, prepare, and consume food, as well as to treat and store water.

Food Storage

In order to prevent wildlife, in particular bears, from acquiring a taste for human fare, it is mandated that all food and scented items be stored in approved bear-resistant containers, especially in Yosemite and at Mt. Whitney. Although some of the camping areas along the JMT provide food lockers, it is not a viable option to cover the entire distance of the trail. Consequently, you will be required to carry your own bear canister throughout your journey.

Bear canisters can be rented from select outdoor stores in California, directly from some manufacturers, and from most wilderness permit offices. Check the respective rental agreement terms, especially regarding returning the canister via mail. For instance, most permit offices (except Yosemite) expect in-person returns. Any canisters offered for rent will usually be approved models, but it is best to double check just in case. The most common rental model is the Garcia, which is used by permit offices.

When purchasing a new or used bear canister, there are a few things to look out for. First and foremost, the canister must be national park approved (SIBBG for black bears, IGBC for grizzly bears). Below is a list of the currently approved models (per NPS/YOSE website):

- Garcia model 812 (Backpacker)
- BV 100b, 200, 250, 300, 350, 400, 450, 500 (Bear Vault)
- Weekender MKII & Expedition MKII (Wild Ideas Bearikade)
- The Bear Keg (Counter Assault)
- Contender 101 & Champ 202 (Bare Boxer)
- Little Sami & Big Daddy (Lighter 1)
- No-Fed-Bear (UDAP)

! As of this writing, the increasingly popular Ursack is not an approved method of food storage along the JMT. For more details on this, visit the respective national park and national forest websites.

The second most important selection criterion is the canister's storage capacity. Depending on your resupply strategy, you will want to get the smallest/lightest canister for the maximum number of days you will be carrying food for. For example, if you plan a 21-day journey with two resupplies, then your bear canister should hold up to seven days' worth of food. To ensure all of your resupply rations (minus the treats) fit into your canister, try packing everything in it prior to sending out the packages.

Apart from their size/capacity, the above-listed canisters primarily vary in weight, transparency, locking mechanism, and price. Table 25 below compares four of the approved models with a capacity of 615-703 cubic inches (10-11.5l). With very good preparation and packing, a canister of around 700 cubic inches (11.5l) can hold food for up to 9-10 days.

Feature	Lighter 1 Big Daddy	Bear Vault BV 500	Backpacker Garcia 812	Bearikade Custom 703
Total Weight	2lbs 11oz / 1.22kg	2lbs 9oz / 1.16kg	2lbs 12oz / 1.25kg	2lbs / 0.9kg
Interior Volume	650 cu. in. / 10.5l	700 cu. in. / 11.5l	615 cu. in. / 10.1l	703 cu. in. / 11.5l
Diameter x Height	8.7 x 13 in. / 22.1 x 33cm	8.7 x 12.7 in. / 22.1 x 32.3cm	8.8 x 12 in. / 22.4 x 30.5cm	9 x 11.25 in. / 22.9 x 28.6cm
Housing Material	poly-carbonate	poly-carbonate	ABS polymer	carbon fiber
Transparent	yes	yes	no	no
Access	tool-free	tool-free	tool required	tool required
Price	$100	$75	$70	$300

Table 25 – Bear Canister Comparison[6]

[6] Information retrieved from respective manufacturers' websites.

The Big Daddy and BV 500 are both made of transparent polycarbonate, allowing you to see what's inside and where it is – a very convenient feature. Both also have lids that *do not* require a tool/coin to unlock. The BV 500 has a screw-on lid with a click-lock mechanism that requires some well-aimed pressure to open. The Big Daddy uses a couple of small screws. The Garcia 812 and the Bearikade have lids that require a coin or similar tool to open. Make sure the locking mechanism is still intact when buying a used canister. The Garcia Cache 812 is simple and cost effective. The Bearikade canisters can be custom-ordered in many sizes. They are handmade of carbon fiber composite material, making them the lightest but also most expensive canisters on the market.

! As a reminder, bear spray and other deterrents are prohibited in several national parks, including Yosemite and SEKI. Proper use of a bear canister and keeping your campsite food- and odor-free should be precaution enough. Save the weight of carrying a spray that could harm both you and the wildlife and get you fined.

Stove & Fuel

The preparation of your meals will undoubtedly require a stove, as campfires are generally less convenient and, more importantly, prohibited in certain areas along the JMT (see Section 3d). There are two basic stove-fuel systems most commonly used by backpackers: disposable gas canisters and refillable liquid fuel canisters. Both are suitable for the JMT.

Disposable Gas Canisters

Disposable gas canisters are filled with a pressurized gas mix of isobutane and propane. They have a self-sealing valve at the top and a thread, which can be used to mount a stove directly onto the top of the canister, using it as a base. Gas canister stoves are extremely light (< 3oz/85g) and pack very small.

Stoves can also be connected to the gas canister via a fuel line. This way, the canister can be turned upside down (also referred to as "inverting"). This allows the canister to operate in liquid feed mode, which eliminates the need for the gas to vaporize inside the canister (which is necessary in case of the top-mounted option). By avoiding the need for vaporization, the gas can be used at lower (sub-evaporation) temperatures without losing performance. This is particularly useful in colder conditions. In addition, placing the stove directly on the ground improves pot stability and makes wind shielding easier.

Figure 24 – Canister Stove Options: Top-Mounted and Fuel Line

A third pressurized gas set up is the integrated canister system. These systems have an integrated burner and heat exchanger, which are directly attached to the bottom of a pot for optimal heat transfer. The entire unit is then mounted onto the top of a gas canister (similar to option 1). Integrated canister systems are well-shielded against wind, and their pots are often insulated to minimize heat loss. As a result, these compact units are especially efficient for boiling water. However, they tend to be more expensive, heavier, and cannot be used with other pots.

In general, all disposable gas canister systems are easy and fast to use, as they do not require priming. They burn cleanly and reach their maximum heat very quickly, and there is little to no risk of fuel spillage. On the downside, the gas canisters are rather expensive and gauging how much fuel is left is difficult. Upright-mounted canisters have a risk of tipping over and their performance can decline in cold weather and as canisters empty and gas pressure decreases. At least for summer trips, canister stoves are very well-suited for the JMT if they contain a propane-isobutane mix. With an operating temperature limit of 21°F (-6°C) at sea level and approximately 1°F (-17°C) at 10,000 feet (3,000m) elevation, they will provide reliable heat along the trail. Liquid feed canister stoves offer additional low temperature range.

ⓘ Keep in mind, the fuel temperature is key not the outside temperature. When confronted with very cold conditions, store your canister inside your tent or even close to your feet in the sleeping bag to ensure that the gas temperature is a few degrees above its boiling point.

Refillable Liquid Fuel Canisters

Refillable liquid fuel stoves have a similar setup to liquid feed gas canister systems. The burner is placed on the ground and connects via fuel line to the bottle fuel tank, which has a pump to pressurize the fuel and a valve to control flow. Most systems require priming, especially in cold conditions. Priming means that a few drops of fuel are placed into a dish underneath the burner and then lit. This heats the attached fuel line, causing the fuel to vaporize and pressing into the actual burner where it can be ignited. Liquid fuel systems are dominated by white gas (a.k.a. naphtha). This is a highly refined fuel with little impurities, so it burns very clean. There are also multi-fuel stoves that run on white gas, kerosene, diesel, and gasoline.

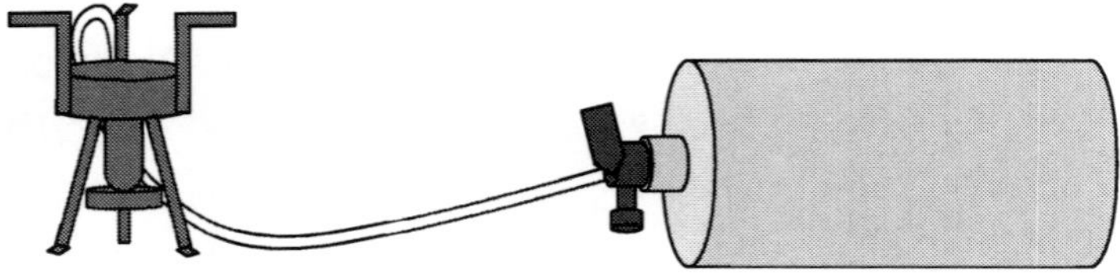

Figure 25 – Liquid Fuel Stove

Generally, the greatest advantages of a (petroleum-based) liquid fuel stove are the easy international availability of its fuels, their low cost, very high heat output, and their ability to operate at low temperatures. White gas, for example, freezes at -22°F (-30°C) to which the stove is operable. Downsides are that some fuels are odorous, smoke, and may blacken pots. The stoves, especially multi-fuel versions, are rather expensive. Furthermore, flames are not as finely adjustable for simmering foods. Operation (including pumping and priming) needs some practice and bears the risk of flare-ups or burns, and stoves require regular maintenance to avoid clogging (all the more, the less purified the fuel is). All this requires some experience and commitment.

Regarding weight, liquid fuel systems are heavier than gas canisters due to the more complex burner and pump-valve system for the bottle tanks. In addition, commonly used pressurized gases have an approximately 5% higher energy density than petroleum fuels. However, liquid fuel tanks are reusable and can be filled as needed, whereas gas canisters are only sold in a few sizes, making incremental adjustments to fuel supplies difficult.

ⓘ Regardless of the type of gas and setup you prefer, don't forget to obtain a free *California Campfire Permit* if you intend to operate a camp stove within the National Forest sections of the JMT.

Fuel Calculation

Another very important question is how much fuel to carry. Unless your meal plan requires special preparation, your fuel consumption will be directly proportioned to the amount of water you need to boil per day. A good approximation of how much fuel is needed to boil water is 0.012oz fuel per ounce of water (11.5g fuel per liter). If certain meals require simmering after the water has boiled, add 0.035oz (1g) of fuel per minute of cooking time.

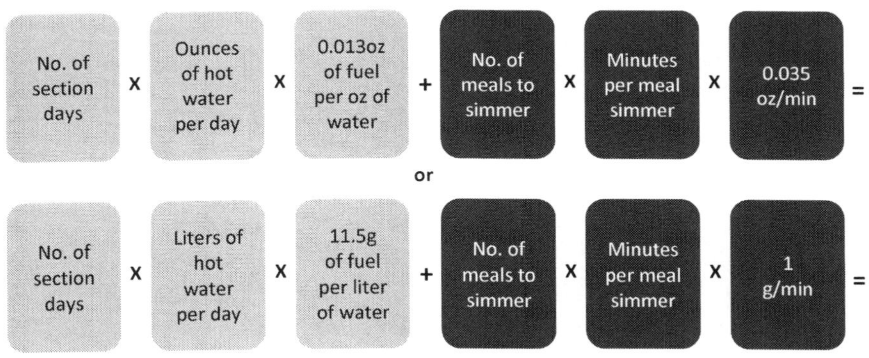

Figure 26 – Estimating Fuel Needs

Figure 26 above shows the equation used to estimate fuel consumption for the duration of your trip. Remember to include all side trips and think about which fuel tank sizes or gas cartridges are best suited to provide sufficient energy while minimizing weight.

Sample Scenario:

Anna is planning 15 days on the JMT with one resupply after 8 days, i.e., her first section is 8 days and her second is 7 days long. Her estimates for hot water demand per day are as follows:

	8 oz.	for coffee in the morning
+	8 oz.	for porridge/oatmeal
+	0 oz.	for lunch
+	16 oz.	for a meal in the evening
+	8 oz.	for one cup of tea
=	40 oz.	of boiling water per day

Five of her first section meals each have to be simmered for 10 minutes. The rest of her meals are dehydrated/instant meals that do not require simmering. Consequently, her fuel estimates for section one and two are:

1) (8 x 40oz x 0.012oz/oz) + (5 x 10min x 0.035oz/min) = 5.6oz
2) (7 x 40oz x 0.012oz/oz) + 0 = 3.4oz

So in total, Anna will need approximately 9 ounces (255g) of fuel for the entire trip. She can now decide if she wants to pack a large enough canister that is going to last the entire trip or if she wants to pack a smaller cartridge first and then resupply or purchase extra fuel along the way.

ⓘ In order to keep boiling times and fuel consumption low, always cover your pot with a lid and start on a small flame, gradually increasing gas flow as water gets warmer, never turning to full throttle. Furthermore, use a screen or heat reflector around your stove and pot to shield the flame from wind.

Lastly, don't forget to bring proper means to ignite a flame. Options include gas lighters, matches, piezo igniters, and spark strikers. Opt for something that is durable, long-lasting, reliable, and water-resistant. Bring at least one redundant option as a backup in case your first choice gets wet or breaks.

Pots, Pans, and Utensils

Deciding what type of pot and/or pan to bring depends on how many people you will be cooking for and what you will be cooking. For example, if you are cooking for 1-2 people, one pot of approx. 32 oz. (0.9l) suffices. Most backpacking meals tend be soup- or stew-like in consistency and can work with a fairly narrow pot. If you intend to prepare solid meals, you may want to opt for a pot or pan with a wider base. Remember to choose cookware that has an easy-to-clean, non-stick surface.

Whether you are cooking liquid or solid meals, materials such as aluminum or titanium help save pack weight, and using a lid speeds up the cooking time while conserving your fuel. Since pack space will be limited, look for a pot or pan that has a foldable or detachable handle and can be stacked inside other cookware. These features will be pretty standard on any cookware sets that are specifically designed for backpacking. Some are even designed to fit a fuel canister inside to help reduce pack space even further.

ⓘ If your cook set is only a single pot, you may also want to consider bringing a small cup/mug (with or without a lid) for hot beverages at camp. This can double as a measuring cup for food preparation and should be extremely lightweight and compact.

While planning your trail meals, it helps to think about and set aside the utensils it will take to prepare them. The standard minimum is usually a spoon or "spork" (spoon and fork in one) and a pocket knife. Long-handled spoons are particularly convenient when eating directly out of the freeze-dried meal pouches or the pot. If your meals require stirring or flipping on the stove, make sure your utensil is heat-resistant.

Water Purification

As discussed earlier in the book, it is advised to treat any water along the JMT before drinking. There are six options for doing so: micro-filter pumps, micro-filter gravity and squeeze bags, ultra-violet (UV) sterilization pens, chemical tablets/drops, and boiling. Choosing a water treatment system is just like choosing any other piece of gear – a tradeoff between features, cost, and weight. Below is a brief summary of some of the most relevant differences between the methods:

- Pump filters are fast and work well even in little, murky water, but they are rather heavy and require some maintenance.
- Gravity filters are fast and easy to use. The clean tank can double as a hydration pack, but they are expensive and rather heavy.
- Squeeze filters are fast, light, cheap, and can filter large amounts of water per cartridge (life span of over 10,000 l/cartridge). However, squeezing is strenuous, and the pouch can easily tear or puncture if squeezed too hard.
- UV lights often come as a pen or integrated in a bottle. They are light, rather fast, and can treat viruses. They rely on batteries to work and need somewhat clear water to be effective.
- Chemical options are chlorine dioxide, sodium dichloro-isocyanurate, and iodine tablets or droplets. They are very light and cheap, and can treat viruses. They are slower than other options and less effective in murky water. Plus, a slight chemical aftertaste usually remains. Also, the individual tablet dosage should match your drinking container size. Some tablets are for two liters of water and are hard to break.
- Boiling water should only be a backup option. It is slow, heavy (including the fuel needed), and leaves you with boiling water to quench your thirst in warm conditions.

Table 26 below summarizes the features and pros/cons of the different water treatment options.

Feature	Boiling	Chemical	UV Light	Squeeze	Gravity	Pump
Speed [l/min]	0.2	0.1-0.25	0.7-1.0	1.5-1.7	1.4-1.8	1.0-1.6
Weight [oz]	0.4/l	2-3	4-6	2-5	8-12	10-15
Treats Viruses	yes	yes	yes	no	no	no
Longevity [l]	n/a	80-100	>10k	>10k	1-2k	1-2k
Ease of Use	easy	very easy	easy	medium	very easy	easy
Durability	long	n/a	fair/long	fair	long	fair/long
Cost	40-50 ct/l	10-15 ct/l	\$80-160	\$30-50	\$80-120	\$80-100
Comment	Requires fuel; drinking hot water	Ineffective in murky water; wait time >0.5h; slight chemical taste	Ineffective in murky water; requires batteries/ charging	Hard squeezing can lead to pouch tears; hand strength needed	Best if hung, incl. storage bags; great for groups	Pre-filter filters large particles; requires mainte-nance

Table 26 – Water Treatment Options

Generally, filters treat protozoa, bacteria, and particulate, and they allow instant consumption. Boiling, UV light, and chemical purifiers are effective against protozoa, bacteria, and viruses, but only if the drawn water is almost clear and after waiting a certain treatment time. All options except pumps are of limited applicability in shallow or small amounts of water. However, this is not a big issue since water is usually plentiful along the JMT and typically very clear.

Water Storage

How to store the treated water for convenient and frequent access is worthy of consideration as well. Two options are most common: water bottles and hydration reservoirs.

Practical *water bottle* sizes are 24-48 fl. oz. (0.7-1.4l). Aluminum, stainless steel, and BPA-free plastic are the most used and suitable materials. Features like narrow or wide openings, sealing valves, and straws are a matter of personal preference. Insulated bottles are generally heavier and have less capacity. Bottle caps with loops allow you to attach the bottle to the outside of your backpack with a carabiner. Take the lightest weight bottle you can find.

Hydration reservoirs are bags made of puncture-resistant, durable material that are placed inside your backpack and typically include a drinking tube, allowing you to access the water without stopping to open up your backpack. At the end of the drinking tube is a bite valve to control the flow of water. When not in use, the mouthpiece can be clipped onto your shoulder or sternum strap for easy access. Typical sizes of reservoirs are 67-100 fl. oz. (2-3l). Wide openings make for easy filling and cleaning of the packs. Hang loops allow you to suspend the reservoir inside your backpack.

ⓘ To remove any plastic taste from your hydration reservoir, mix a few tablespoons of baking soda, 34 fl. oz. (1l) warm water, and some white vinegar. Let the mixture sit in the bladder overnight, then rinse thoroughly. After your hike, clean and dry your reservoir thoroughly, then store in the freezer to prevent bacteria from growing.

Choosing a bottle or hydration reservoir is a matter of personal preference. Both options are suitable for the JMT. During my trip, I used a hydration reservoir for the first time. My decision was based on the fact that I was going to use trekking poles and wanted a hands-free drinking option. I also thought I would drink more regularly if water was easily accessible, assuming that good hydration is a basis of endurance. I was very happy with my choice and have since used it on many more hikes. The only downsides are having to remove the bladder from the backpack for refilling and the difficulty of gauging water consumption. Apart from that, bite valves make frequent drinking very easy and storing the large reservoir in your backpack gets you far while distributing the weight evenly on shoulders and hips.

This leads to the question of what size your container(s) should be and how much water to carry in between refill stops. My non-scientific answer is approximately 67 fl. oz. (2l). If you are very weight conscious, you can go with half but will need to look at the trail sections ahead of you. Some passes are dry for over two hours of sweat-intense uphill. Carrying less water, you will also have to unpack your treatment gear more often. You may also want to bring a small (34 fl. oz./1l) backup reservoir to carry extra cooking water for the last stretch while looking for a camp site and/or as an emergency container.

e. Medical & Personal Care

For lightweight enthusiasts, this section may be particularly painful. It deals with bringing several items of which you hope never to use any. Nevertheless, a well-equipped first aid kit is vital in case of emergency. Your personal kit should include any medications you regularly take and those that were recommended to you for this specific trip. There are various pre-assembled first aid kits, however, hikers tend to have different needs and standards regarding personal care when outdoors. Limit yourself to the minimum you feel comfortable with. Below are some suggestions on what to pack:

First Aid – General

- Self-adhesive bandages
- Tape (sufficient for emergency and blisters)
- Antibacterial wipes/ointment

- Non-stick sterile pads
- Self-adhesive elastic bandage wrap
- Scissors or knife
- Pain relieving gels/creams (with Camphor, Menthol, Arnica)
- Anti-inflammatories and/or pain relievers (e.g., ibuprofen)
- Blister treatment (bandages, pads, etc.)
- Acetazolamide for altitude sickness
- Survival blanket (silver/insulated)
- Whistle

First Aid – Specific or Optional

- Any personal medication
- Antihistamines (to remedy allergic reactions)
- Tweezers (for splinters)
- Tick removal tool
- Safety pins
- Insect-sting relief
- Sun relief (e.g., aloe vera)
- Blood thinner (e.g., aspirin)
- Small irrigation syringe (to rinse wounds)

Personal Care

- Sunscreen (SPF 30 and up)
- Lip balm (with SPF)
- Toothbrush & paste
- Insect repellent
- Soap (biodegradable)
- Deodorant
- Moisturizer
- Toilet paper (~1 roll/week)
- Hand sanitizer

f. Miscellaneous

The following gear can be just as important as the gear listed earlier. Many choices are purely subject to personal preference.

Gear	Comment
Camera	When deciding on the right type of camera for your trip, consider the trade-off between weight and photo/video quality. Some hikers choose to bring a full DSLR kit, while others just carry a smartphone. No matter your preference, be sure to bring enough batteries and storage to last your entire trip, as well as a proper case that not only protects your equipment from the elements but also allows quick access.
Compass	A compass is good to have but not essential in the summertime, as trails are well-marked and visibility is usually good.
Fishing Gear	A line and some trout lures are sufficient, but you can also bring a pole. Any fishing requires a valid California fishing license. Unless you are planning a more leisurely trip and are certain that you will fish, leaving these items at home will save extra weight.
Gloves	Whether you are looking for extra warmth or better protection from harmful UV rays, hiking/sun gloves can be a great addition. When using trekking poles, gloves can help reduce chafing on hands.
GPS Watch	GPS watches allow tracking and analyzing of various statistics of your hike (e.g., distances traveled, speed, pace, elevation). They are nice to have to monitor your progress but not essential for navigating.
Light Source	Lighting in the dark is important to think about – for camp preparations in the evenings, early or late hiking, reading in the tent, and going to the bathroom at night. Most hikers carry a headlamp because it allows them to have both hands free. This aspect is

	particularly important when attempting to climb Mt. Whitney at night to watch the sunrise. Be sure to pack enough batteries to last your entire trip.
Map/Map App	See Section 3a for available JMT maps/map apps. Be sure to download any electronic maps to your smartphone completely before setting out, since data coverage along the trail is spotty at best.
Money/ID	Bring some cash and a credit card for food, public transportation, hitch hiking, postcards, emergency, etc. Also bring a driver's license or other official form of identification to pick up permit.
Rope	Nylon parachute cord is perfect to hang clothes for drying or to replace a strap on the backpack or a broken shoelace. Make sure it is not too thick.
Satellite Messenger	Useful to communicate with family and friends during your trip and to call for help in case of emergency, since cell phone service is not reliable.
Solar Charger & USB Power Bank	The sun is a reliable source of energy on the JMT. To capture it, there is a variety of solar chargers and USB power banks to choose from. Make sure that any device you plan to take has the correct specs to charge all of your electronics.
Sunglasses	Essential to protect your eyes from harmful ultraviolet (UV) rays, especially at higher altitudes. Your sunglasses should block 100% of UV light. Polarized lenses are a great feature to reduce glare.
Towel	Quick-drying, synthetic fabric, lightweight.
Trowel	Useful to bury human waste. Choose one that is light but sturdy, as the ground can be rocky and tough.

Table 27 – Miscellaneous Gear Items & Comments

7. Personal Experience

In this chapter, I describe my personal preparations, travel arrangements, gear choices, and experiences along the trail. It is the summary of the trip I completed with my good friend, Josh, and meant to exemplify what has worked for us. It offers only my personal experience and opinion. If you are a less experienced hiker and/or unsure about certain choices and options, I hope this will give you some additional reference points.

a. Plan

Logistics

As a first step, I researched the JMT and decided in which direction to walk it. We chose north-to-south, because a) we trusted the majority of hikers' opinion and b) we wanted to ascend Mt. Whitney without having to deal with the lottery system when entering from Whitney Portal. About four months prior to our intended start date, I checked for available permits online at the NPS/YOSE website, called the wilderness permit office, and faxed the application. I received confirmation of my trail entry date the same day, also via fax. I then made a reservation for a one-way rental car to drive from San Diego to Merced two days before our entry date. For Merced, we booked a motel near the small airport, where both the rental car drop-off and the bus station of the YARTS to Yosemite Valley are located. The YARTS did not require a reservation. Since we were going to start our trip in busy July and did not get a permit for the Happy Isles trailhead but Glacier Point instead, we were faced with the decision of either hiking up a steep incline from the valley floor to Glacier Point or take a bus. We decided to take a bus, worried our packs would be insanely heavy in the beginning. Consequently, I also made the required reservation for the Glacier Point charter bus. We printed out all of our confirmations and marked on a map how to get everywhere and by when. This concluded the long lead items for me. Since the idea of hiking the JMT came from Josh, my hiking buddy was already fix.

Gear

With the logistics taken care of, I had about four months leading up to the trip in order to research, buy, and test gear. I'm like a kid in a candy store at a good outdoor shop. I frequently dropped by, tried out products I had researched online, and kept an eye out for deals – both in-store and online. When people at the register started greeting me by my name, however, I was starting to wonder if I was going overboard – and began monitoring my bank account more closely.

I had a decent backpack and what I thought was a good sleeping bag, but still needed quite a bit of gear. What I was most unsure about before the trip was what to expect in terms of temperature and how to prepare for sleeping arrangements. I couldn't quite believe the numbers from the temperature charts, thinking it was impossible it would get that cold in California during the summer. On the other hand, I found it difficult to gauge in online forums, who the "normal" hikers were and who the "minimalist" ultralight backpackers with a latent death wish. Talk of not needing a tent and sleeping under the stars sounded appealing but also risky. In hindsight, I would consider both Josh's and my approach to be very average/common for the trail and fitting for most people's comfort levels. Here is a list of my gear:

Gear	Comment
Backpack	75 liters, rather rugged (i.e., heavy but durable), well-padded and ventilated. I used the sleeping bag compartment for my bear canister – not an ideal weight distribution, but very convenient access. Map was in the top pocket, sunscreen accessible on the side, and the drinking tube clipped to a loop on my right shoulder strap so it was always within reach. Josh had an equally rugged, but poorly ventilated pack. He had never encountered any problems with it, but was sweating more under the California sun and soon faced issues with chafing along his hips and shoulders. Also, his

	pack had less compartments and pockets, making it more difficult to organize gear/find what he was looking for.
Tent	1-person, 3-season, ultralight tent with a footprint. Packed weight just over 2 lbs. (1kg). I highly recommend using a modern, lightweight 1-person tent over a bivy bag. The extra weight is nothing compared to the additional comfort. Before the trip, I was thinking about saving weight and using a tarp if I had to. I am very glad I didn't. There might be experienced hikers for whom that is a feasible option, but it definitely wasn't for me. Josh used an older bivy. It weighed about as much as my tent, but since he already owned it, he thought he'd save the extra $250. Overall, it worked ok. At each campsite, he would collect a few rocks and sticks to expand the bivy as far out as possible, allowing more air circulation. This was the biggest issue, as the bivy had a single shell of waterproof, non-breathable material. Josh could not keep his backpack dry under the vestibule like I did, nor could he move around much, let alone change clothes in his bivy.
Sleeping Bag	Ultralight down bag with a comfort zone of 54°F (12°C). It was far too cold! I would opt for a comfort zone of at least 40°F (4°C).
Sleeping Pad	Ultralight, minimalist frame air pad, which is designed to cushion only the body parts that touch the ground when lying flat (head, shoulders, butt, calves, feet). It was far too cold and uncomfortable, especially if you prefer to sleep on your side, in which case your hip bone will soon hit the ground. There are other excellent lightweight options out there. I now own a very comfortable air pad that is 2.5 inches (6.3cm) thick and only weighs 12 ounces (350g).
Stove	Simple, 4-arm-foldout camp stove that is mounted on top of gas canister – worked great.
Fuel	Gas cartridge with isobutane mix – easy handling, worked great. Between the two of us, we used one 8 oz.

	(227g) canister per week. We heated water for hot muesli and coffee every morning and had hot water for tea and dehydrated meals every evening. I was, however, very cautious about gas consumption, keeping the flame low, the lid on, and using a wind shield.
Lighting Device	Spark striker – works great and is absolutely reliable, but we also had one backup lighter.
Pot	Together, we shared one coated pot with a capacity of approx. 34 oz. (1l). The pot had handles that folded to its sides and a lid. It was cheap and absolutely sufficient.
Long Spoon/ Utensils	We both had one plastic spoon that was about 9 inches (22cm) long. It worked great for scraping muesli out of the pre-packed zip lock bags and eating straight out of the dehydrated meal pouches. That's all we needed.
Bear Canister	700 cu. in. canister. We both used a transparent one with a screw-click lid and bought them when they were on sale. They are not very light, but rather inexpensive, work fine, and double as a seat.
Water Treatment	Squeeze filter system. The pros included its good flow rate and light weight. The cons were that the rubber seal between filter and pouch kept getting loose, blocking the thread, falling into the pouch, or simply not sealing well. Also, the pouch had several holes at the end, squirting water everywhere and making refills quite time consuming. I would recommend either a lightweight pump (can be shared by multiple people) or iodine tablets/droplets. As a backup, I carried some tablets anyway which weighed less than 1 oz. (30g).
Hydration Pack	70 fl. oz. (2l) hydration pack with a non-insulated drinking tube. Along the trail, there is never a reason to carry more than 70 fl. oz. (2l). While carrying less water is viable, it requires more planning, stops, and unpacking a filter - so this size seemed perfect for Josh and me.

Extra Foldable Reservoir	34 fl. oz. (1l). A spare water reservoir comes in handy at camp and should your hydration pack tear. It is also convenient for washing up with soap away from lakes and streams. The extra weight is negligible.
Mug with Lid	16 fl. oz. (0.5l) plastic mug with a tight-fitting, sippy-cup lid. The mug kept my tea and coffee warm for a long time and had water measurement lines. Great!
Pocket Knife	Swiss army knife with scissors. A knife is a must. Additionally, the scissors came in very handy when cutting tape and bandages.
First Aid Kit	I compiled my own first aid kit with antiseptic, bandages, plenty of tape, blister pads, ibuprofen, and tiger balm. Each evening, I applied tiger balm to my knees and ankles, which sometimes act up. Throughout the trip, I was pain free and the smell was refreshing before going to bed.
Silver Survival Blanket	We each carried one survival blanket that we spread beneath our sleeping pads for extra insulation. With both my sleeping bag and pad being inadequate, I was thankful for any extra warmth. In case of other emergencies or shelter, a survival blanket is versatile and weighs little.
Sunscreen	I used one 2 oz. (60ml) tube of SPF 30 per week. I only used sunscreen for my neck and face, occasionally for my arms. Wearing long sleeves, high collars, and other textiles is always favorable over sunscreen. The combination of dust, sweat, and sunscreen gets ever more uncomfortable throughout the day.
Soap	One 1 oz. (30ml) bottle of biodegradable soap was more than enough for me. Since we only used the pot for boiling water, there was nothing to clean but ourselves and our spoons.
Camera	Though it was painful to hike amidst such beautiful scenery without my SLR, I did not bring it. I do not regret

	my decision, because I know the SLR's extra weight, bulkiness, and fragility would have annoyed me on the trail. Instead, I brought a good point-and-shoot model, two 32GB SD cards and two extra batteries – all three batteries were empty at the end. The batteries did not work in the mornings when it was too cold. Keep them in your sleeping bag or carry the battery separately in a pant pocket in the morning for quicker warming up. I got a small neoprene case with a belt loop that I attached to my hip belt so it would not slide out. This way, my camera was protected and always within my immediate reach. I highly recommend this.
Map or Map App	I used the Tom Harrison 13-page topographical maps. The maps are durable and detailed enough to navigate along the trail.
Elevation Profile	An elevation profile with a vertical mileage chart is very helpful to plan your daily distances. I had gathered different elevation profiles from posts online. None were really great – that's why I made my own for this book. I had set out to hike the JMT in 14 days, which meant approx. 16 miles per day. I roughly marked camping spots every 16 miles along the elevation map and then moved them back or forth a little, depending on each stretch's elevation. This gave us a rough guideline of where we needed to be after each day. In the evenings, I would reassess and plan the next day, but overall we stuck to our original itinerary rather closely.
Money	I hadn't planned on stopping for food or buying anything at the resupply. But after an evening of soaking in the hot springs, we treated ourselves to breakfast at Red's Meadow Resort and got some snacks at the store next door. At the resupply, we did not purchase anything – we had too much gas to begin with and more food than we could carry. After 221 miles at Whitney Portal, burgers and a beer were too tempting to resist. Finally, our return to San Diego was free. All in all, about $40 in cash were sufficient for me.

Rope	I had brought plenty of rope along that I never used. On the second to last day, my shoe lace did rip, but I was able to re-tie it. 15 ft. (5m) of 3-5mm emergency rope should suffice.
Shovel	We bought and shared a cheap ($3) plastic shovel. It was light but broke at the end. The shovel could have been ok with more caution while digging, but a sturdy model is definitely a plus. As with everything, it is a question of what you are willing to spend.
Sunglasses	My shades were rubberized on the inside and fit fairly tight, making them sit nicely without sliding. Look out for 100% UV protection. Polarized lenses are a plus, mine brilliantly intensify colors.
Toilet Paper	We each used about one role per week, but each had one role extra. TP is not something you want to have to substitute. Estimating your usage and pack accordingly.
Towel	I brought a small synthetic, quick drying towel of approx. 15x20 inches (40x50cm). It is perfectly sufficient for drying off after a swim and will dry quickly.
Solar Charger & LED Lamp	Instead of a flash light or headlamp, I only brought a LED light with a USB port that connected to my solar charger. The 7 LEDs are very bright but energy efficient. My solar charger with battery, only 3x5 inches (8x12cm), powered the LEDs for over 4 hours. In the evenings, that was far more than we needed. Only on our last ascent to Mt. Whitney, leaving camp at 4 AM, I got close to - but never depleted - its full capacity. While Josh had his headlamp strapped on, I put my charger in my top backpack pocket and let the LEDs shine over my shoulder. The lights were attached to a flexible metal hose of approx. 6 in. (15cm), so I could adjust the light to shine right in front of me.
Trekking Poles	As stated earlier, I strongly advocate trekking poles. I used extendable telescope poles with one clip and one twist lock. Make sure to always secure the locks tightly. My poles have shock absorbers. To me, they are neither

	a big gain nor harm. Well-fitting and moisture-wicking grips are far more important, as are fitting straps and the right length adjustment.
Fishing Gear	Excited about the possibility of adding fresh fish to our trail menu of dried goods, I acquired a CA fishing license and brought some fishing gear. Keeping it lightweight, I ditched pole and reel and only packed some line on a spool, flies, and bobbers. We only fished twice and caught one presentable trout. If you are hiking the JMT in 14 days or less, you should have quite a pep in your step to be able to spare time for fishing.

Table 28 – Personal Gear Items & Comments

Food & Resupply

Nutrition plays a major role in completing the JMT successfully. In addition to the suggestions given in Section 5b, here are some personal remarks on the food we brought:

Meal	Comment
Breakfast	We had muesli every morning, each individually packaged in a durable (freezer) zip lock bag. I bought a variety of oats, grains, granola, nuts, seeds, coconut flakes, and dried fruit and made variations for each day. Each serving consisted of 2 generous cups of pre-mixed muesli, half a cup of powdered milk, and two table-spoons of protein powder. When hiking, I feel I crave stronger tastes and flavors. Variations of flavor can be achieved with flavored granola (strawberry, blueberry, maple, etc.) and/or instant oat-meal (peach, cinnamon apple, cherry, etc.). Personally, I could eat muesli every day for the rest of my life and be happy with it, but some might like a bit more variation. Especially for hiking, I found that mixing your own muesli lets you combine a variety of great, nutritious ingredients and precisely control your intake.

Lunch	Preparing lunches was the most difficult, I found. We mainly had flat tortillas or pumpernickel, either with dried & smoked sausage, fish in a pouch, or peanut butter. I personally got tired of the sausage after day one. While it was nice to have something salty, it was too much for me. Fish pouches were great, and I refined them with spices or small sachets of hot sauce. Peanut butter is definitely very nutritious but equally fatty. Though I love a PB&J sandwich, I am not a fan of large quantities, especially without jelly. All in all, the lunches I planned had too little variety and rarely seemed very appealing. However, I also found that I simply wasn't very hungry in the midday sun.
Snacks	We both really enjoyed chocolate protein bars and other granola bars in a variety of flavors. Dried apricots, apples, and other fruit are also great, but rather heavy. Almonds and nuts are nutritious and come in different flavors (roasted, etc.) but tend to dry out your mouth. We generally didn't snack as much as I had assumed. One snack per day was sufficient, being either one bar or a small handful of fruits or nuts.
Dinner	Dinners were as simple as they were great. Prior to the trip, I had bought a few dehydrated meals from different brands and tested them on short hikes. They were all enjoyable, and one brand tasted especially delicious to me. There are far more varieties than days on the JMT, so you can have a different meal every evening. Their preparation is also very simple. The only downside is the price at $7-10 per pouch. However, for Josh and me, the taste and convenience after a long day of hiking outweighed the cost. It was definitely worth it, I would highly recommend them.
Condiments	Each morning, we either had a hot coffee or tea. We premixed instant coffee with creamer and sugar – not gourmet but got us going. Sugar tasted especially delicious on the trail. In the evenings, we had ginger and herbal teas – a great way to warm up.

	If you are taking self-prepared meals, it would definitely be good to bring some extra spices, olive oil pouches, or similar. Our dehydrated meals didn't need seasoning, but hot and other sauces added some variety to our lunches.

Table 29 – Personal Food Strategy & Comments

As you can conclude from my comments, I was very happy with our breakfast, snack, and dinner options, just not with the smoked sausages and lack of variety for lunch. However, as for quantities, 2.5-3.5 ounces (70-100g) are a good amount of meat or fish per day. Overall, I can recommend a similar pack list if you substitute four of the sausage portions with jerky, different fish, or vegetarian options.

Our resupply package I sent out so that it would arrive a good week before we would pick it up. We planned only one resupply at Muir Trail Ranch, about halfway to Mt. Whitney. Aiming to complete the JMT in 14-16 days, we each started off with 8 days' worth of food, plus a little extra food for emergencies. Additionally, we carried one day of extra food outside of the bear canister that we ate at Yosemite the day before our trip. For resupply, we sent a good 8 days' worth of food, plus extra goodies, such as apples, wine in a carton, coconut water, chocolate, and ready-to-eat tortilla stuffers, as well as essentials like sunscreen and toilet paper.

Figure 27 – Organizing Resupply Food and Bear Canister

We organized our food by trail sections. Figure 27 above gives you an idea of how we tried to spread out and sort the four 8-day sections worth of food between the two of us. Each horizontal row represents one section for one person and consisted of eight daily rations, including breakfast, lunch, snacks, and dinner. Puncturing and letting all air out of our freeze-dried meal pouches, we each just managed to squeeze one section's worth of food into our 700-cubic-inch bear canisters.

This is exactly what we packed per person per trail section:

Meal	Our Food	Quantity
Breakfast	Muesli variations	8 freezer zip lock bags, each with 2 cups of Muesli mix, ½ cup of milk powder, and 2 tbsp. protein
Snacks	Granola, fig, and protein bars	8 bars, mixed variety
	Nuts & dried fruit	4 cups (½ cup per day) of nuts & dried fruit mix
Lunch	Smoked & dried sausage	6 portions of 3.5 oz. (100g) each
	Salmon & tuna in pouches	2 pouches, 2.5 oz. (70g) and 3 oz. (85g)
	"Carbs"	1 pack of 8 large tortillas 20 oz. (550g) 1 pack of pumpernickel 18 oz. (500g)
Dinner	Dehydrated entrees	8 pouches of 4-6 oz. (110-170g) each
Extra Food	Sausage & peanut butter	1 portion of sausage 2 packs of 1 oz. (30g) peanut butter

Table 30 – Personal Food Pack List

b. Go

Our adventure began two days before our entry date in Yosemite. It was exciting to finally execute on the months of planning. We picked up our rental car (credit card needed at pick-up!) in the morning and drove from San Diego to Merced. At the motel, we took a dip in the pool and walked across the street for one of our last fresh meals. We savored a fresh salad and speculated about what lay ahead. The next morning, we drove the short distance to the Merced Airport and returned our rental car. With some time to spare, we weighed our packs at the airport check-in counter: 43 lbs. (20kg) without water. Lugging them the short distance from the airport to the bus stop already seamed so strenuous we briefly forgot why we thought doing this for 221 miles was a good idea.

Figure 28 – Merced Airport and YARTS Bus to Yosemite Valley

Dead on time, the YARTS bus arrived. As this was the route's first stop and there was no one but us, we got front row panorama seats behind the bus' huge windshield. The driver was in a great mood, telling us lots of stories about the area and Yosemite National Park. Much to our amusement, he honked on accident whenever we made a turn – it surprised him each time and never got old to us. With every minute of the 3-hour drive, our suspense grew. After a narrow passage in between granite of which we do not know how the bus fit through, Yosemite Valley opened up. Lush meadows lay sun-drenched at the bottom while water cascaded and fell over the steep walls to the sides. At the Yosemite Village bus stop, we grabbed our packs and walked over to the Yosemite Valley Wilderness Center to pick up our permits. The rangers went through the "dos and donts" and a few minutes later we were set. We walked over to the backpackers' campground, set up our tent and bivy for the first time, walked to Mirror Lake and Curry Village (recently renamed to Half Dome Village), had baked beans, and went to sleep.

Figure 29 – Yosemite Valley and Backpackers' Campground

Day 1: July 31, 2013, has finally arrived! We hopped on the Valley Shuttle to Yosemite Lodge and switched over to the chartered bus. The 1.5-hour drive out of the valley and back up took us to Glacier Point, an awesome overlook of Yosemite Valley and right opposite of Half Dome. There was not a cloud in the sky, but smoke from wildfires near Mammoth covered the scenery in a haze that thickened in the distance. After countless but barely sufficient photos from the lookout spots, and a mental image of the last indoor restroom for a long time, we officially began our journey. Glacier Point is the start of Panorama Trail. With spectacular views, the Panorama Trail joins the JMT 3.3 miles (5.5km) after its Happy Isles Trailhead, just before crossing the Merced River at Nevada Fall. Few day hikers get past this point and solitude increases with every mile.

Figure 30 – Glacier Point and Nevada Fall

With blue skies and around 90°F (30°C), the California sun was challenging our strength from early on and the smoky air wasn't helping either. Likewise, it took some time to fine-tune and get used to the weight and gear. Adjusting backpack straps properly and tightening shoes adequately takes some playing around with. Also, my trekking poles felt a little strange at first, timing and placing of feet and pole tips seemed a little uncoordinated. But around the second or third day, the motion became completely natural and the poles felt like a great support.

Day 2 introduced us to the beauty and hardship of the JMT. Headed north, we passed small pines and crumbling rocks on our way to Cathedral Lakes. We were feeling the effects of the heat, smoke, and altitude as we approached the top of Cathedral Pass, at 9,700 feet (2,900m). But the gradual descent thereafter eased the strain. 5 miles (8km) past Tuolumne Meadows, we camped near the Lyell River. Steam was rising from the water, while deer, marmots, chipmunks, and a pheasant awaited nightfall. Dark blue turned black as one star after the other came out until the entire sky was star-studded. Evening two was magical. However, as the clear air turned crisper, humidity settled on our tents. With temperatures dropping below freezing, I lay awake shivering until I finally decided it was time to rise at 6:00 AM. As I squirmed out of my sleeping bag, I was stunned to notice it was securely frozen to the side of the tent. The tent itself was covered in small ice crystals, as was the surrounding meadow.

Figure 31 – Clear Skies and Frozen Grass at Lyell River

Day 3 gave us a rough start. With Lyell Canyon being rather narrow, we would have waited quite a while for the sun. So at 6:30 AM, we packed our wet stuff and got moving – our only way to warm up. After two hours of walking along the stunningly beautiful river, we spread our tents and sleeping bags on flat slabs of rock and had breakfast. Within 20 minutes, the sun and wind had thoroughly dried our gear and we could continue. It was around 9:00 AM and, by this time, the thought of previously having felt cold already seemed absurd. After a few more miles of flat terrain, the ascent to Donohue Pass began. Steps and switchbacks took us from 9,000 feet (2,700m) to over 11,000 feet (3,300m), all in the brutal midday sun. Additionally, smoke from Mammoth lingered in the air without a breeze. Getting enough oxygen felt strenuous at times. Nonetheless, traversing the first pass over 11,000 feet (3,300m) was exhilarating and the view of the surrounding peaks and snow patches was most rewarding.

Figure 32 – Drying Gear and Marmot at Donohue Pass

These first days confirmed three important lessons: (1) do not camp too close to bodies of water, (2) do not camp in basins, and (3) try to choose your campgrounds so that you have an incline early in the morning.

Day 4 – Falling behind already?! Our campground near Rush Creek was roughly at the 40-mile mark from Yosemite's Happy Isles. With a 16-mile-per-day schedule, we had fallen 8 miles behind in only 3 days. We justified the gap with getting adjusted to trail life and some tough conditions caused by the smoke. We were optimistic to make up the time and distance lost. Another approach would have been to alter the mileage if you think your initial assumptions on the drawing board do not match the trail's reality, as exit dates are non-binding. At 6:00 AM, we began to make up ground. Our morning hike was spectacular. Under the slightest of clouds, we passed a series of crystal-clear lakes that mirrored the surrounding sharp peaks and snow patches. Each of the Thousand Island, Emerald, Ruby, and Garnet Lakes was gorgeous and tempting to spend time at.

Figure 33 – Thousand Island Lake

But we pushed on through, nonstop from 10,000 feet up and down to 7,500 feet. At the northern cut-off, we paralleled the JMT to check out Devils Postpile. Then, after a respectable 20-mile day, we pounded our stakes in the ground and submerged in the hot springs at Red's Meadow Campground. Though the temperature was painful at first, the heat quickly relaxed our muscles and deeply calmed all senses. Thoroughly heated to the core, I had my first shiver-free night.

Day 5 called for luxury. After the amenity of discarding some of our waste in the campground trash cans and using a proper bathroom, we had a gourmet breakfast with fresh fruit, French toast, and bacon at Red's Meadow Resort. At the store next door, we sent out postal life signs to our spouses and stocked up on survival blankets to fight the cold. We re-joined the JMT to continue on and regain the 2,500 feet we had lost the previous day. While the air was only approximately 60°F (15°C), the sun felt especially merciless along the dusty switchbacks through previously burnt forests. Near a junction, I asked a lady in her mid-50's if she could show us where we were, while presenting her my paper map. She replied, "Ya, just hold on a sec.", pulled out her smartphone with a JMT app, and showed me our exact location. I felt quite outdated as we continued. The sky had turned dark orange as we arrived at Lake Virginia. We jumped straight into the perfectly clear water, briefly destroying its flawlessly smooth surface. With a small glass of Whiskey, we sat by the shore watching trout jumping, deer cautiously grazing, and butterflies fluttering. As daylight faded, the mirrored images disappeared from the lake's surface while stars drew new ones in the sky.

Figure 34 – Late Evening Reflections on Lake Virginia

Day 6 took us over the 10,895-foot (3,321m) Silver Pass and its beautiful lake with sandy shores all the way down to Mono Creek at 7,870 feet (2,400m). The campground near the Vermilion trailhead was the busiest we stayed at. It is located just beneath the switchbacks leading up to Bear Ridge. We had heard horror stories about how strenuous this section was supposed to be. Nevertheless, as we ascended in the morning of day 7, we found it quite enjoyable. Most of the path is well shaded in a lush forest, and the morning temperatures eased the countless but steadily inclining zig-zags. Around Marie Lake, we bumped into a gentle cowboy leading eight mules. He was carrying gear and food for a group of hikers. After the incredibly steep granite switchbacks leading down to Lake Edison, I told him I would freak out if I had to do all this on a horse. He replied he would freak out if he had to carry a backpack and eat dried food for three weeks. His dinner the night before was grilled chicken with green beans and a beer. With 35 years of experience going back and forth on the JMT, he reassured us the best was yet to come: "You ain't seen bulls**t!"

Figure 35 – Silver Pass and Pack Mules

Day 8 was resupply day. Our morning began in the beautiful pine forests around the picturesque Sallie Keys Lakes. Mice like it here, too. A few of them decided that the cup Josh had left out overnight would be a good place to leave some droppings. Josh had previously read about the prevalence of the Hantavirus in the area, a virus transmitted mostly by rodent excrement and leading to potentially lethal diseases. After thoroughly disinfecting the cup with boiling water and rubbing alcohol, we made sure never to leave anything outside again and got on our way. After some switchbacks, we took the cut-off to Muir Trail Ranch and crossed San Joaquin River. With some effort, we found the scenic lake and the adjacent hot spring in the middle of the high-grassed Shooting Star Meadow. While the water was rather murky, the temperature was perfect for soaking. All washed up, we headed over to Muir Trail Ranch where our resupply packet was waiting for us. Along with several other hikers, we spread our food on one of the tables and started sorting. On the one hand, we hadn't finished all our food yet, because we had packed one day's worth of extra food. On the other hand, we had sent ourselves too much resupply food. After leaving behind some good food in the cache bins for following hikers and handing out chocolate to everyone around, we continued. We were now approximately at the 107-mile mark – halfway to Mt. Whitney!

The fact that the resupply worked well was great, but it also meant we upped our pack weight by about 12 lbs. (5kg) from one moment to the next. However, the anticipation of the treats we had just packed propelled us. And the first one didn't survive long. Among others, we had sent four fresh apples, and we each ate one just after we continued our hike, strongly craving fresh food. Near Goddard Creek junction, we set up camp next to large slabs of west-facing rock. After washing up, we each took out a 500ml carton of red wine from the resupply, lay on the warm rock, and enjoyed cheese pretzel appetizers. As our spirits were lifting, darkness crept in, bats flew from tree to tree, and occasional shooting stars enchanted the evening. We fell asleep outside full and happy.

Figure 36 – Hot Spring in Shooting Star Meadow and Resupply at MTR

Day 9 – Evolution and Elevation. Our day began with switchbacks leading out of Goddard Canyon. The trail was magnificent, running right along Evolution Creek, which cascaded over rocks, collected in pools, and gently ran on as it sparkled, reflecting the bright morning sun. Evolution Valley opened up to a wide pine forest with grazing deer. Throughout the day's steady incline, the shade from the trees was well-appreciated. Switchbacks took us ever higher and along lakes, of which one was more pristine than the next. With each lake and level of elevation, the vegetation and scenery changed. Tall pines were replaced by short ones, then by various shrubberies, until we had reached Wanda Lake at 11,426 feet (3,483m) with nothing but a few grasses growing at its edges. After crossing the 11,955-foot (3,644m) Muir Pass, we had to walk past Lake Helen, where all campgrounds were occupied, and continue for a daily total of 18 miles (29km), until we dropped at 7:30 PM.

Figure 37 – Deer in Evolution Valley

Day 10 lost and regained equal elevation. In the morning, we walked along beautiful rivers and side streams down to Le Conte Canyon. Among lush meadows with deer and babbling brooks, we found the ranger station at Bishop Pass junction. We got some updates from the ranger, especially that fires were no threat to us, and pieces of chocolate chip cookies from his wife. They were heavenly, we couldn't thank her enough. Alongside Palisade Creek, we hiked up the almost white rock of the narrow canyon to the upper Palisade Lake. Here, we invited Keith and Nichole to have dinner with us, the father and daughter we had been bumping into almost daily since we camped next to them at the backpackers' camp in Yosemite. We each prepared our meals and then traded Tequila and fig bars for dessert. Keith told us the story of how he had started to hike the JMT 29 years ago and now returned with his daughter to finish it – a wonderful evening in the company of interesting fellow hikers.

Figure 38 – View from Mather Pass

Day 11 was our lunar landing. A steep incline of over 1,000 feet (300m) took us to Mather Pass and over 12,000 feet (3,658m) for the first time. The view up there was spectacular: barren peaks, bright gravel, and scattered rocks as far as the eye could see. Descending into the Upper Basin, we stood-out among the wide fields of unvegetated rocks like men on the moon. By lunch time, we had hiked down almost 3,000 feet (900m) only to climb straight back up again over the 12,130-foot (3,697m) Pinchot Pass. We shared the peak experience with a group of boy scouts who were somewhat surprised as we took off our shirts and waved our flags in the air – Josh additionally pulling his pants to his ankles. We had done this routine at every peak and pass on the trail, although never in company.

Day 12 – A mini vacation. After a breakfast conversation with Keith and Nichole who had set up their tents close to ours, the JMT took us through two insanely gorgeous canyons. Both Woods Creek and South Baxter Creek were stunning – water cascaded gently over flat rock, bubbled in round pools, and dropped down cliffs to have its spray sparkle in the sunlight. We had lunch at Dollar Lake and then only hiked three more miles before picking a campsite at Rae Lakes. It was merely 2:30 PM. Usually, we had hiked until at least 6:00 PM. But the setting was too wonderful: steep slopes rose out of the water, surrounding the lakes, while scattered flat patches were sheltered by large boulders and pine trees, making perfect campsites. We enjoyed a short siesta, took a swim, and then emptied Josh's bear canister to use it as a washing machine drum. By now, repacking the food was no longer an issue and by far outweighed the convenience of this method. Sitting on one of the boulders at the lake with just some line and a fly, we were able to land a decent-sized trout. We served the fish appetizers along with a small glass of Whiskey while reclining on a warm rock and gazing at the clouds. It was yet another of many perfect moments on this trip.

Figure 39 – Rae Lakes

Day 13, we headed on to Mars. Reenergized from our mini vacation, we crossed over 11,978-foot (3,651m) Glen Pass as if it was nothing. On the other side, we bumped into a couple from Canada that decided to exit the JMT via Kearsarge Pass and gave us some extra food and gas. With that, we had a fancy warm lunch in Vidette Meadow and continued. By 6:00 PM, we were an hour away from 13,180-foot (4,017m) Forester Pass and looking for rest. However, the mostly steep and open terrain at around 12,000 feet (3,658m) wasn't inviting. So we pushed over the pass and landed on Mars. The view was phenomenal. At this late hour, the sun had the peaks glowing bright red. Nothing but red shimmering pebbles, rocks, and boulders lay intimidating in front of us. Accompanied by countless marmots squeaking on their hind legs, we descended for almost an hour until we reached the first patch of trees and level ground for camp. By now, all the energy we had recharged the day before was gone, and we were cooling off quickly. With little sunlight left, we walked to the nearest creek. Washing up was especially unpleasant in the cold wind. We filtered water for our hydration packs and took some extra water for cooking in our spare pouches. As soon as the food and hot tea were done, I excused myself and sought shelter in my tent. Looking at the map, I realized we had hiked two passes and a total of over 18 miles (29km) that day. We were now in a position to finish the JMT on the 15th day.

Figure 40 – Glen Pass and Mars Landing

Day 14 – Recapping the adventure. As I got out of my tent, I was just as cold as when I had gotten in the night before. But the mood quickly brightened as the sun came out over Bighorn Plateau. Scattered, weather-beaten tree stumps with beautiful wavy grain turned into patches of lush pine forests that were periodically interrupted by, again Mars-like, sterile red pebble deserts. Under 11,000 feet (3,353m), vegetation picked up as we hiked along wet meadows. This morning was another good example of how varied and interesting the sceneries along the JMT are. At 3:00 PM, we had passed Guitar Lake and pitched our tent next to the lake above it. After relaxing and a quick swim, we lay on a flat rock facing west, overlooking Guitar Lake's shimmering surface. As the sun slowly set in the distance, sending beams of pink and orange our way in between the peaks, we recapped our adventure. Time had both flown by and felt endless. We were thankful everything had gone so smoothly. With the last drops of Whiskey Josh had been carrying for over 200 miles now, we discussed our strategy for Mt. Whitney and got ready for our final ascent.

Figure 41 – Watching the Sunset at Guitar Lake

Day 15 – Exhilarated at the highest peak of the contiguous United States. We got up at 4:00 AM, packed our stuff and began climbing. In utter darkness, Josh used his headlamp while I had my LED-solar-charger-combo tucked in my top backpack pocket and shining over my shoulder. After about 1,500 vertical feet (457m) from our campsite, we reached the Mt. Whitney cut-off where you could leave your pack and ascend along the ridge. From here, the view over Guitar Lake to the mountains around is magnificent, especially as you witness the sun slowly lifting dusk with shades of light blue and violet until it bursts out in blazing orange and red.

At 7:35 AM on August 14, 2013, we had reached the peak of 14,505-foot (4,421m) Mt. Whitney, the highest point in the contiguous U.S. The feeling of joy and accomplishment was second to none. The steady inclines and passes over 12,000 and 13,000 feet in the past days had given us time to acclimatize well, validating the decision of hiking the JMT north-to-south. After absorbing the views and emotions, we signed the register and hit a big red button someone had left beside the book. "That was EASY!", said the talking button before we shut the lid to the register and began our descent from 14,505 feet to 8,365 feet (2,550m), nonstop. Though very beautiful, we were only focused on finishing this last steep part accident-free and completing the trail.

Figure 42 – Sunrise on the Way to and on Top of Mt. Whitney

At 3:15 PM, we sat in front of a burger and a beer at Whitney Portal, saying cheers. 221 miles (356km) now lay behind us. Keith and Nichole also arrived, as did Bob, a soft spoken 64-year-old who had solely eaten cereal and power bars on the trail, the infamous "Bob-bars". With our first non-dehydrated meal in 10 days in our belly, we got cleaned up, bought a souvenir T-shirt, and took our thumbs to the street. After receiving multiple offers but none going south, we accepted a couple's suggestion to take us down to Lone Pine and try our luck there. After only 15 minutes at the side of the main street, Josh called me over, standing next to an enormous luxury RV on a nearby parking lot. I declined his waiving. The sight made all my alarm bells go off, and I had flashbacks from bad horror movies.

Josh, however, was already taking his shoes off and climbing onboard. Turns out, the driver of the RV, John, used to hitchhike a lot himself and said to his wife Kathy, "Wait 'till you see those guys' faces when we give them a ride in this thing." John was right, and our surprise didn't end there. As we sat on the fluffy couch, Kathy handed us a cold beer, fixed a fruit and vegetable platter, and finally a rum and coke. I wasn't sure if this was really happening. Neither was my wife Nadja who drove three hours from San Diego to pick us up where John and Kathy dropped us off. Nadja was standing in the parking lot as our huge RV drove up, steps slid out automatically, the door opened, and two bearded versions of ourselves greeted her with big smiles. In the restaurant nearby, we began piecing together the exhilarating impressions of our extraordinary adventure!

Figure 43 – Saying Goodbye to Mt. Whitney and the High Sierras

Appendices

A. Trail Overview Map

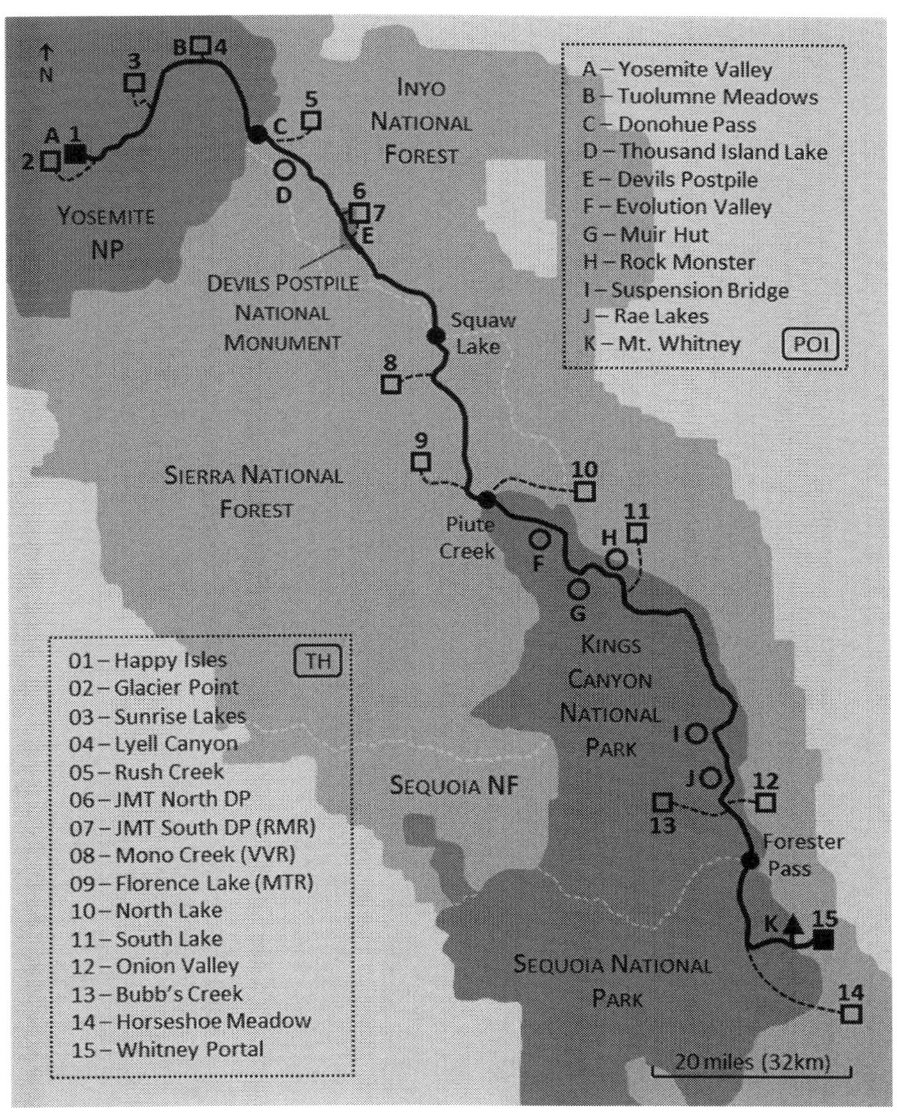

N
A 1
2
3
B 4
5
C
D
6
7
E
Yosemite NP
Inyo National Forest
Devils Postpile National Monument
Squaw Lake
8
9
10
11
Sierra National Forest
Piute Creek
F
G
H
Kings Canyon National Park
I
J
12
13
Sequoia NF
Forester Pass
K
15
14
Sequoia National Park
20 miles (32km)
A – Yosemite Valley
B – Tuolumne Meadows
C – Donohue Pass
D – Thousand Island Lake
E – Devils Postpile
F – Evolution Valley
G – Muir Hut
H – Rock Monster
I – Suspension Bridge
J – Rae Lakes
K – Mt. Whitney
POI
01 – Happy Isles
02 – Glacier Point
03 – Sunrise Lakes
04 – Lyell Canyon
05 – Rush Creek
06 – JMT North DP
07 – JMT South DP (RMR)
08 – Mono Creek (VVR)
09 – Florence Lake (MTR)
10 – North Lake
11 – South Lake
12 – Onion Valley
13 – Bubb's Creek
14 – Horseshoe Meadow
15 – Whitney Portal
TH

B. Elevation Profiles

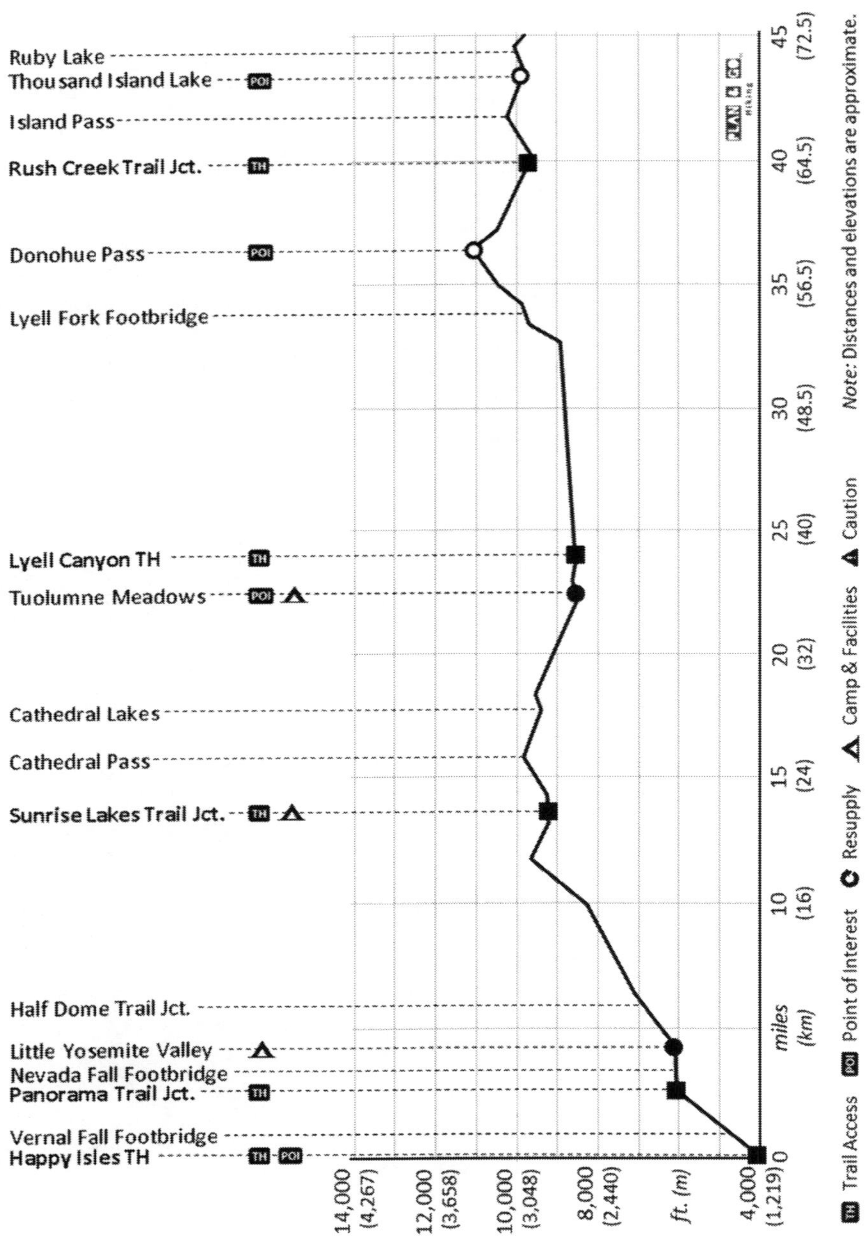

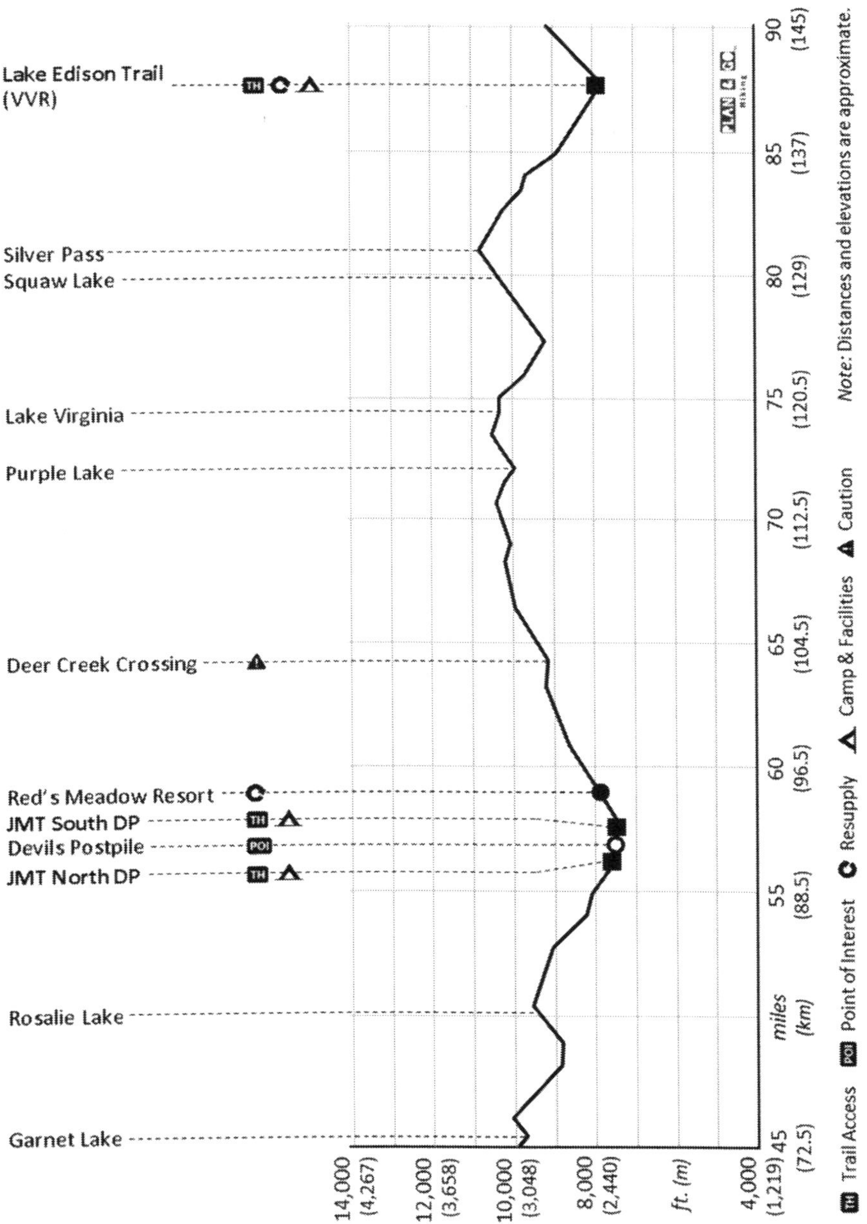

Lake Edison Trail (VVR)
Silver Pass
Squaw Lake
Lake Virginia
Purple Lake
Deer Creek Crossing
Red's Meadow Resort
JMT South DP
Devils Postpile
JMT North DP
Rosalie Lake
Garnet Lake
14,000 (4,267)
12,000 (3,658)
10,000 (3,048)
8,000 (2,440)
ft. (m)
4,000 (1,219)
miles (km)
45 (72.5)
55 (88.5)
60 (96.5)
65 (104.5)
70 (112.5)
75 (120.5)
80 (129)
85 (137)
90 (145)
TH Trail Access
POI Point of Interest
Resupply
Camp & Facilities
Caution
Note: Distances and elevations are approximate.

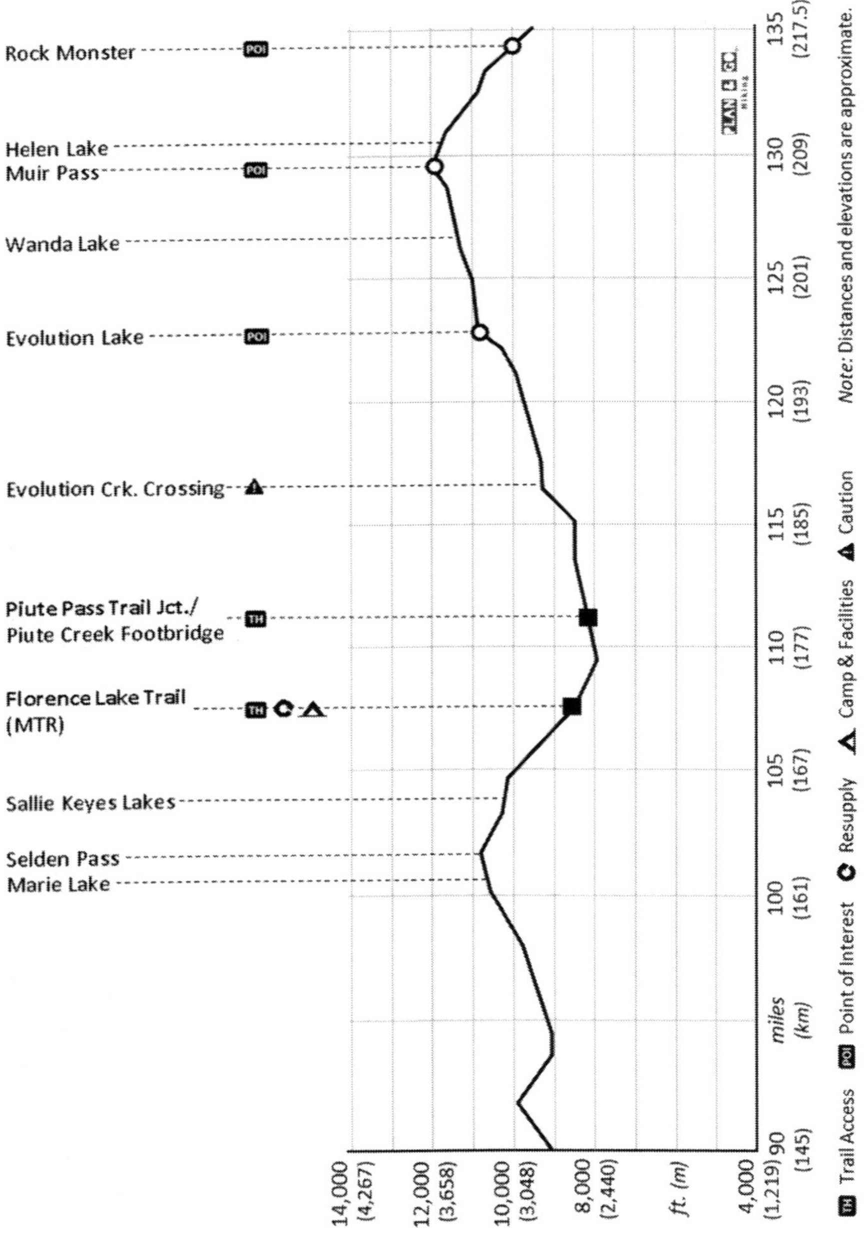
Rock Monster
Helen Lake
Muir Pass
Wanda Lake
Evolution Lake
Evolution Crk. Crossing
Piute Pass Trail Jct./
Piute Creek Footbridge
Florence Lake Trail
(MTR)
Sallie Keyes Lakes
Selden Pass
Marie Lake
POI
TH
14,000
(4,267)
12,000
(3,658)
10,000
(3,048)
8,000
(2,440)
ft. (m)
4,000
(1,219)
90
(145)
miles
(km)
100
(161)
105
(167)
110
(177)
115
(185)
120
(193)
125
(201)
130
(209)
135
(217.5)
TH Trail Access
POI Point of Interest
Resupply
Camp & Facilities
Caution
Note: Distances and elevations are approximate.

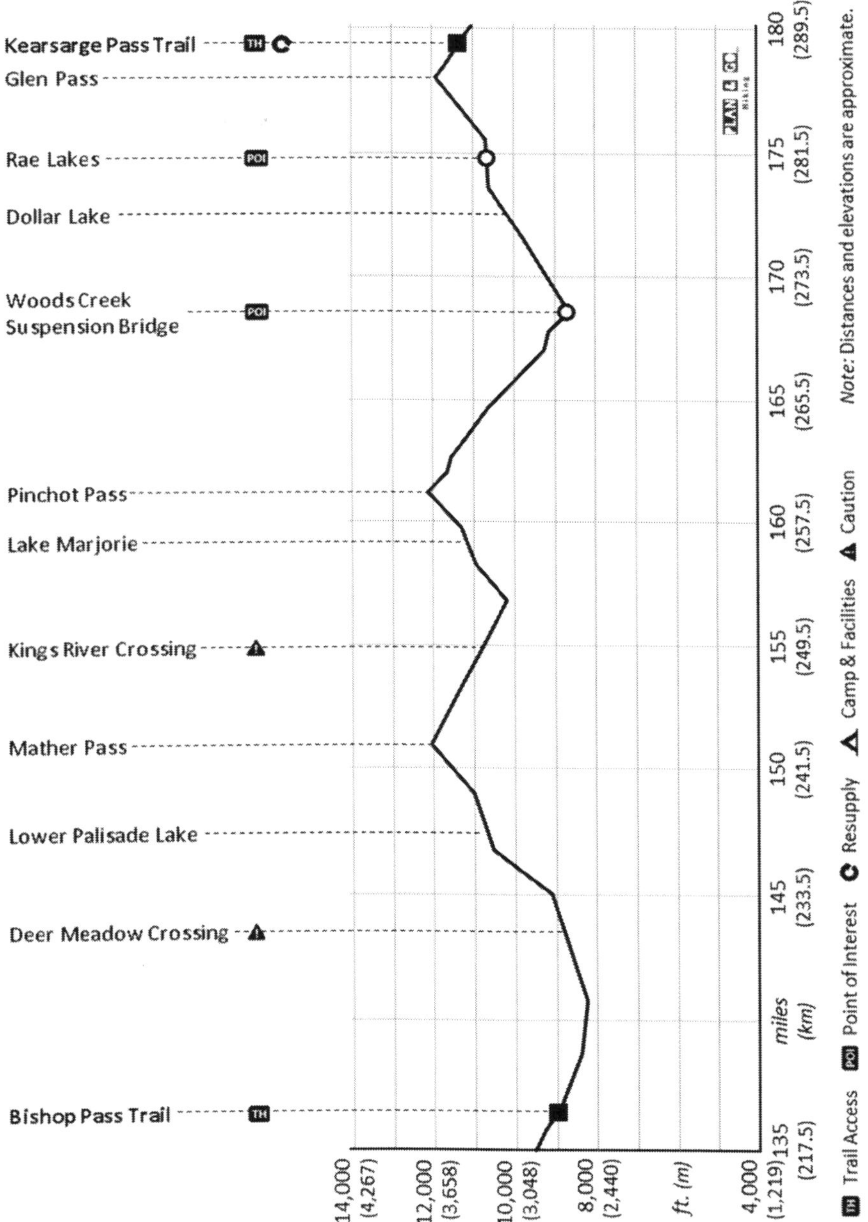
Kearsarge Pass Trail
Glen Pass
Rae Lakes
Dollar Lake
Woods Creek Suspension Bridge
Pinchot Pass
Lake Marjorie
Kings River Crossing
Mather Pass
Lower Palisade Lake
Deer Meadow Crossing
Bishop Pass Trail
TH
POI
14,000 (4,267)
12,000 (3,658)
10,000 (3,048)
8,000 (2,440)
ft. (m)
4,000 (1,219)
miles (km)
135 (217.5)
145 (233.5)
150 (241.5)
155 (249.5)
160 (257.5)
165 (265.5)
170 (273.5)
175 (281.5)
180 (289.5)
TH Trail Access
POI Point of Interest
Resupply
Camp & Facilities
Caution
Note: Distances and elevations are approximate.

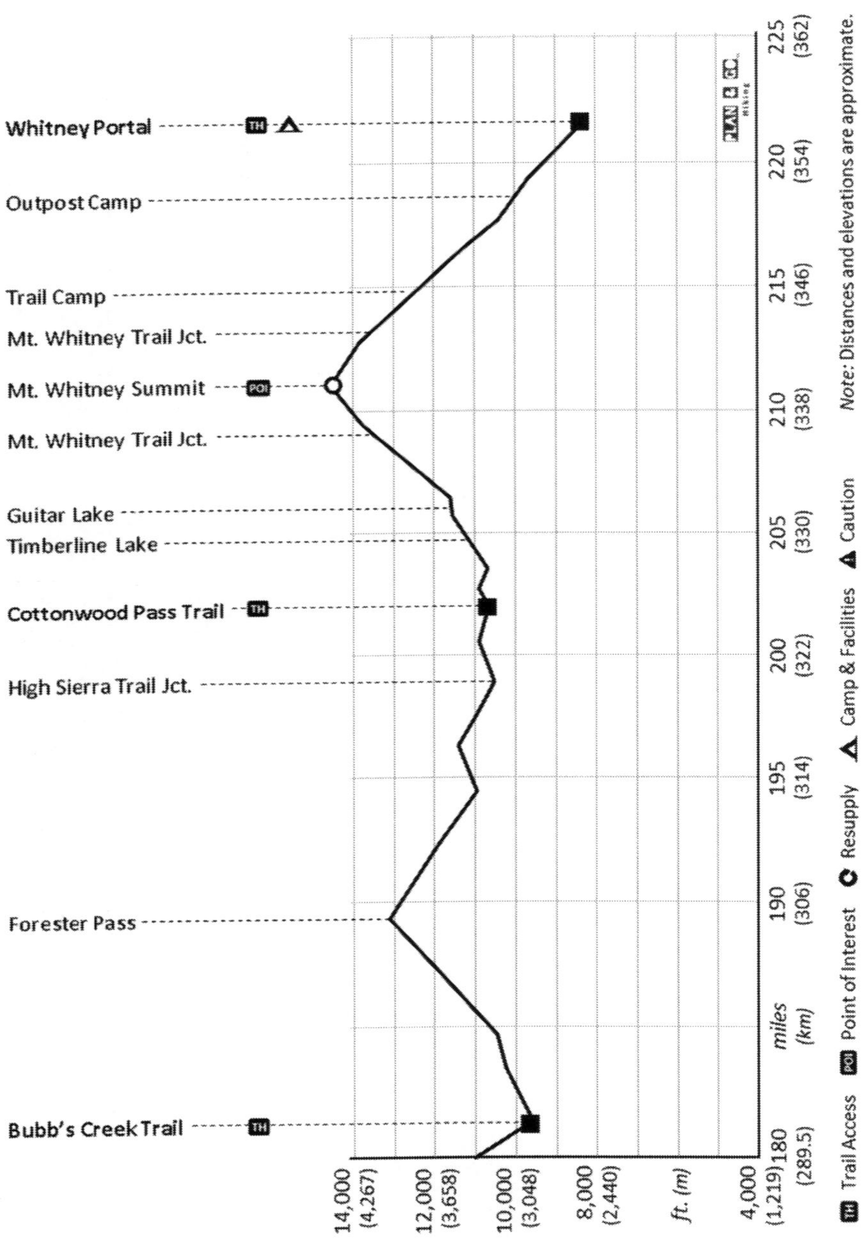
Whitney Portal
Outpost Camp
Trail Camp
Mt. Whitney Trail Jct.
Mt. Whitney Summit
Mt. Whitney Trail Jct.
Guitar Lake
Timberline Lake
Cottonwood Pass Trail
High Sierra Trail Jct.
Forester Pass
Bubb's Creek Trail
TH
POI
14,000 (4,267)
12,000 (3,658)
10,000 (3,048)
8,000 (2,440)
ft. (m)
4,000 (1,219)
180 (289.5)
miles (km)
190 (306)
195 (314)
200 (322)
205 (330)
210 (338)
215 (346)
220 (354)
225 (362)
Trail Access
Point of Interest
Resupply
Camp & Facilities
Caution
Note: Distances and elevations are approximate.

C. Campsite Locations

Section 3d discussed the rules and regulations for overnight camping along the JMT. There is plenty of opportunity to set up camp in locations that meet these requirements, so you should have no trouble identifying suitable sites when planning your personal itinerary. To get you started, below is a list of established or previously impacted campsites that are well-placed in terms of access to water, exceptional scenery, and strategic location. These sites and many others can be easily identified using the topographic map or online mapping tool of your choice.

SB (mi)	NB (mi)	Campsite	Elev. (feet)	Bear Box	Camp Fire
0.0	221.1	Designated Backpackers' Campground in Yosemite Valley ($6 per person, first-come, first-served); toilets	4,000	Yes	Yes
4.2	216.9	Camping area in Little Yosemite Valley; composting toilet	6,125	Yes	Yes
6.5	214.6	Many sites near Sunrise Creek, just a short distance past Clouds Rest trail junction; view of Half Dome to the west	7,230	No	Yes
13.0	208.1	Camping area near Sunrise High Sierra Camp (free of charge, first-come, first-served); toilet, water tap	9,335	Yes	No
17.6	203.5	Several sites along shore of Lower Cathedral Lake; follow side trail for 1/2 mile	9,340	No	No
22.5	198.6	Designated Backpackers' Campground at Tuolumne Meadows ($6 per person, first-come, first-served); toilets	8,600	Yes	Yes
28.0	193.1	Camping in Lyell Canyon is permitted once you pass the landslide area, approx. 4 miles beyond Tuolumne Meadows	8,865	No	Yes
33.2	187.9	Many sites a short distance east of Lyell Fork Footbridge; if this area is too crowded, continue south for about 1 mile until you reach a small lake (Lyell Fork headwaters)	9,670	No	No
42.9	178.2	Several sites along shore of Thousand Island Lake (no camping within 1/4 mile of lake's outflow)	9,845	No	No

SB (mi)	NB (mi)	Campsite	Elev. (feet)	Bear Box	Camp Fire
45.3	175.8	Several sites along south shore of Garnet Lake (no camping within 1/4 mile of lake's outflow)	9,760	No	No
50.4	170.7	Several sites along shore of Rosalie Lake	9,440	No	Yes
52.3	168.8	Several sites approx. 1 mile south of Gladys Lake	9,550	No	Yes
56.6	164.5	20 sites at Devils Postpile Campground ($20 per night, first-come, first-served); flush toilets, potable water	7,650	Yes	Yes
57.3	163.8	52 sites at Red's Meadow Campground ($22 per night, first-come, first-served); flush toilets, potable water	7,620	Yes	Yes
59.0	162.1	Red's Meadow Resort & Pack Station	7,700	No	No
64.8	156.3	Many sites around Deer Creek	9,125	No	Yes
72.3	148.8	Several sites near Purple Lake	9,950	No	No
74.3	146.8	Several sites approx. 1/4 mile north of Lake Virginia	10,400	No	No
83.5	137.6	Several sites along Silver Pass Creek	9,550	No	No
87.9	133.2	Tent campsites at Vermillion Valley Resort (first two nights are free of charge, first-come, first-served)	7,890	Yes	Yes
96.2	124.9	Several sites between trail and Bear Creek, approx. 1/2 mile north of Hilgard Branch	9,190	No	Yes
107.7	113.4	Muir Trail Ranch	7,600	No	Yes
111.2	109.9	Several sites on eastern side of Piute Creek, just past the footbridge	8,090	No	Yes
115.1	106.0	Many sites between San Joaquin River footbridge and switchbacks to Evolution Valley, just 1/4 mile past Goddard Canyon junction	8,485	No	Yes
119.1	102.0	Several sites near McClure Meadow; views of The Hermit and Mt. Darwin to the southeast	9,645	No	Yes
125.1	96.0	Several sites along shore of Sapphire Lake	11,020	No	No
132.9	88.2	Several sites at Starr Camp; views of Black Giant, Langille Peak, and Le Conte Canyon to the south/southeast	10,400	No	No
135.3	85.8	Many sites in Big Pete Meadow	9,250	No	Yes
143.6	77.5	Many sites in Deer Meadow	8,875	No	Yes

SB (mi)	NB (mi)	Campsite	Elev. (feet)	Bear Box	Camp Fire
147.2	73.9	Several sites southeast of Lower Palisade Lake; view of Mather Pass to the south	10,780	No	No
152.3	68.8	Several sites on both sides of trail in Upper Basin	11,490	No	No
158.0	63.1	Several sites near Bench Lake/Taboose Pass trail junctions	10,820	No	No
168.1	53.0	Many sites southeast of Woods Creek crossing	8,540	Yes	Yes
172.8	48.3	Many sites along shore of Arrowhead Lake; view of Fin Dome to the south	10,325	Yes	No
174.3	46.8	Many sites along shores of Rae Lakes; view of Painted Lady to the south	10,590	Yes	No
181.9	39.2	Several sites in Vidette Meadow	9,530	Yes	Yes
184.2	36.9	Many sites near Center Basin junction	10,465	Yes	No
194.0	27.1	Several sites near Tyndall Creek crossing, just a short distance north of Tyndall Creek trail junction	10,940	Yes	No
198.5	22.6	Many sites south of Wallace Creek crossing	10,400	Yes	No
203.4	17.7	Many sites near Crabtree Ranger Station; pit toilet	10,660	Yes	No
205.9	15.2	Many sites along north shore of Guitar Lake; views of Kaweah Peaks to the west and Mt. Whitney to the east	11,500	No	No
214.8	6.3	Several sites at Trail Camp; little to no shade	12,015	No	No
218.4	2.7	Many sites at Outpost Camp	10,360	No	No
221.1	0.0	25 sites at Whitney Portal Campground ($22 per night, reservation required); additional tent sites at nearby Mt. Whitney Trailhead Campground (one-night stay limit, first-come, first-served)	8,340	Yes	Yes

D. Section Hikes

Devils Postpile to Happy Isles

Distance:	56.8 miles	*Elev. Gain/Loss:*	+8,297/-11,873 ft.
Duration:	4-6 days	*Difficulty Level:*	moderate
Permits:	Inyo NF (www.recreation.gov)		
Notes:	Walking S-to-N avoids Yosemite lottery and Donohue exit quota		

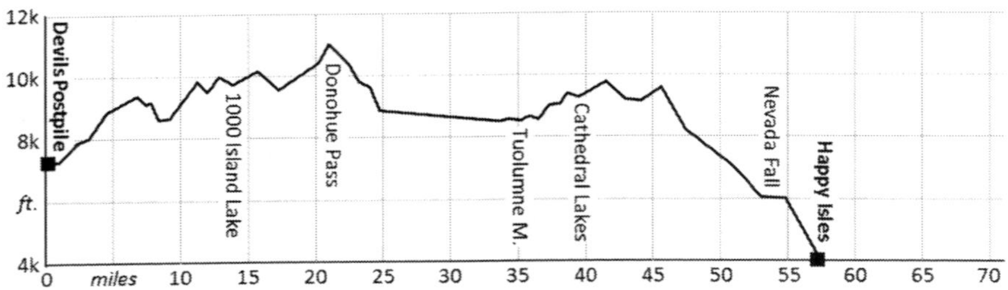

Devils Postpile to North Lake

Distance:	69.2 miles	*Elev. Gain/Loss:*	+13,241/11,522 ft.
Duration:	5-7 days	*Difficulty Level:*	strenuous
Permits:	Inyo NF (www.recreation.gov)		
Notes:	Hot Springs at Red's Meadow Camp & Shooting Star Meadow		

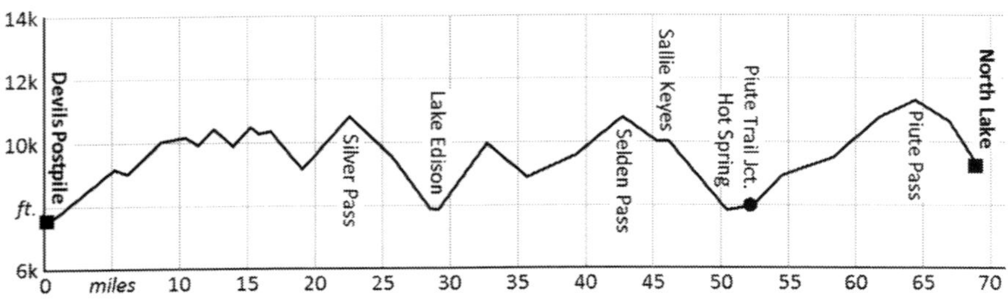

North Lake to South Lake "Loop"

Distance:	52.3 miles	*Elev. Gain/Loss:*	+9,675/-9,229 ft.
Duration:	4-6	*Difficulty Level:*	moderate/strenuous
Permits:	Inyo NF (www.recreation.gov)		
Notes:	Walking between the two trailheads would add ~12 miles		

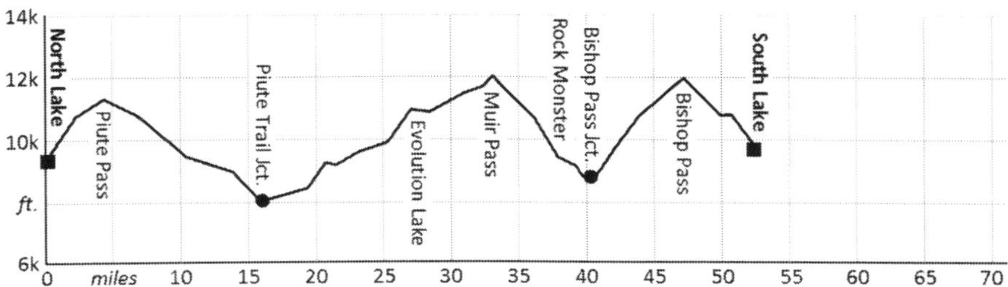

South Lake to Onion Valley

Distance:	61.5 miles	*Elev. Gain/Loss:*	+12,795/-13,383 ft.
Duration:	5-7 days	*Difficulty Level:*	strenuous
Permits:	Inyo NF (www.recreation.gov)		
Notes:	This route will take you over a total of five passes		

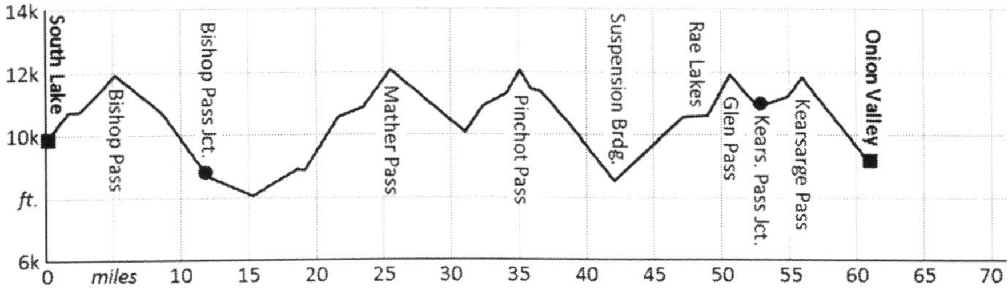

Onion Valley to Whitney Portal (incl. Mt. Whitney Summit)

Distance:	49.0 miles	*Elev. Gain/Loss:*	+11,631/-12,520 ft.
Duration:	4-6 days	*Difficulty Level:*	strenuous/hard
Permits:	Inyo NF (www.recreation.gov)		
Notes:	You will enter the Whitney Zone (see Section 4a for details)		

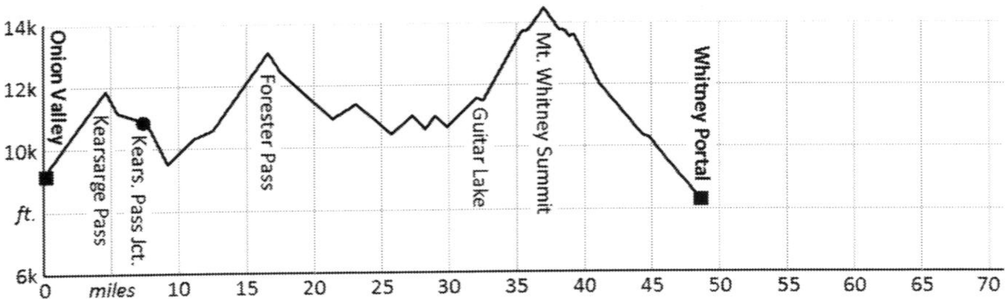

Onion Valley to Horseshoe Meadow (incl. Mt. Whitney Summit)

Distance:	64.7 miles	*Elev. Gain/Loss:*	+14,646/-13,927 ft.
Duration:	6-8 days	*Difficulty Level:*	strenuous/hard
Permits:	Inyo NF (www.recreation.gov)		
Notes:	You will not enter the Whitney Zone (see Section 4a for details)		

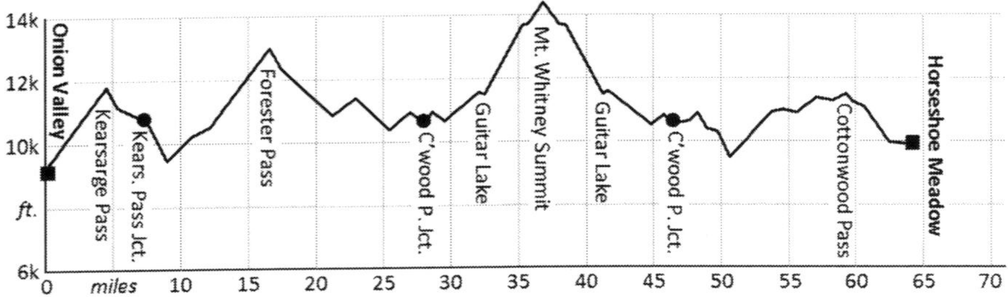

E. Side Trips

There is an infinite number of lakes and peaks to venture out to. With the scenery changing frequently, you will find a more interesting, beautiful, and surprising landscape each day to take in and relish. If your time and planning allow, there are magnificent side trips from the JMT.

Among the most beautiful side trips are:

- **Half Dome** (near JMT SOBO mile 6):
  Yosemite's iconic landmark. Visiting the top of Half Dome takes a 4-mile out-and-back side trip from the JMT, including a steep incline of 400 feet along a cable route. At the top, you'll be treated to spectacular 360-degree views of the High Sierra, including Yosemite Valley and El Capitan.
- **Minaret Lake** (near JMT SOBO mile 55):
  A beautiful lake beneath the jagged Minaret peaks. The Minaret Trail cut-off is located 1.5 miles north of Devils Postpile. From there, it's an approximately 7-mile out-and-back hike.
- **Mount Solomons** (near JMT SOBO mile 129):
  The 13,040-foot peak provides excellent views of much of the High Sierra. It's a short, easy climb from Muir Pass, allowing you to bag a nearby thirteener as part of your JMT journey.
- **Split Mountain** (near JMT SOBO mile 152):
  At 14,065 feet, Split Mountain is a good opportunity to climb another fourteener besides Mt. Whitney. It's easily identified by its two peaks (north summit is highest) and can be accessed from Upper Basin, just a mile south of Mather Pass.
- **Bench Lake & Arrow Peak** (near JMT SOBO mile 158):
  Clear lake with lots of gorgeous peninsulas near Arrow Peak. The 2-mile (one-way) Bench Lake Trail is located opposite from Taboose Pass Junction. Arrow Peak is a solitary peak that rises from the Kings River to 13,809 feet, towering over Bench Lake.

- **Sixty Lakes Basin** (near JMT SOBO mile 175): Peaceful group of lakes in pristine surrounding. The Sixty Lakes Basin cut-off is located in between the Middle and Upper Rae Lakes. From there, a 2.4-mile (one-way) trail leads to the basin.
- **Painted Lady** (near JMT SOBO mile 176): Towering over Rae Lakes, the symmetrical 12,126-foot peak is famous for its multi-colored bands of sedimentary rock.

Any of the trail-adjacent peaks and lakes are included in the JMT permit, with the exception of Half Dome. Due to the large crowds in Yosemite Valley, the trek along the cables up to Half Dome's peak requires a separate permit, which is, unfortunately, hard to come by.

If you plan to start your JMT hike from within Yosemite and would like to climb Half Dome as part of your trip, be sure to mark the respective checkbox on your *Yosemite Wilderness Permit Reservation Application*. Note, however, that this might further decrease your chances of getting the desired JMT permit, since Half Dome permits are very high in demand as well. Visit the NPS/YOSE website for more information.

For all JMT trips originating outside of Yosemite, you will need to apply for a *Day Use Permit* through the pre-season Half Dome lottery during the month of March or the two-day in advance daily lotteries throughout the season, i.e., when Half Dome cables are up (usually mid-May through mid-October). Visit the Recreation.gov website for more information.

View of Half Dome and Yosemite Valley from El Capitan

F. Checklists

These checklists are meant to assist you in your preparations. Depending on the month you plan to hike and your personal preferences, you can add or remove certain items from the lists. For those unsure about what to pack, if you stick to these lists, you will be in good shape.

Clothing ( ) indicates optional items

	Hiking pants/shorts
	Hiking T-shirt (long/short)
	Hiking socks
( )	Sock liners
	Hiking underwear
	Hiking hat/visor
	Neck protection (multi-functional scarf/gaiter)
( )	Belt
( )	Hiking gloves
	Fleece/puffy jacket
	Wind/rain jacket

	Beanie/warm cap
( )	Rain pants
	Warm gloves
( )	Glove liners
	Lightweight camp shoes
	Long underwear top (night)
	Long underwear bottoms (night)
	Spare pair of socks (night)
	Stuff/dry sacks
( )	Swimwear
( )	Clothes for after hike

Hiking ( ) indicates optional items

	Backpack
( )	Rain cover
	Hiking footwear
( )	Leg/ankle gaiters
	Trekking poles
( )	Sunglasses

	Maps/Map App
	Compass
( )	Small shovel
( )	Rope
( )	Mosquito headnet
	Emergency whistle

Sleeping ( ) indicates optional items

	Shelter
( )	Rainfly
( )	Footprint
	Sleeping bag

( )	Compression sack
	Sleeping pad
( )	Silver blanket
( )	Camping pillow

Meal Prep & Hydration ( ) indicates optional items

	Camp stove
	Fuel canister
	Spark striker/lighter/ waterproof matches
	Pot/cookware
( )	Windscreen
	Long-handled spoon
( )	Cooking utensils

	Mug (incl. lid)
	Pocket knife
	Primary water reservoir (bottle/bladder)
	Emergency water reservoir
	Water purification system
	Bear canister
( )	Spare zip lock bags (waste)

Electronics ( ) indicates optional items

	Headlamp/flashlight
( )	GPS watch (incl. charger)
( )	Smartphone (incl. charger)
( )	Satellite messenger/PLB
( )	Camera (incl. case)
( )	Camera tripod

( )	Spare camera batteries
( )	Spare memory card(s)
( )	Camera battery charger
( )	Solar charger
( )	USB power bank
( )	E-book reader

Medical & Personal ( ) indicates optional items

	Toothbrush & paste
	First aid kit
	Personal medications
	Sunscreen
	Lip balm (with SPF)
	Insect repellent
	Toilet paper
( )	Eye mask & ear plugs

( )	Hand sanitizer/wet wipes
( )	Lotion/moisturizer
( )	Small microfiber towel
( )	Notepad & pen
	ID & money
	Travel docs (printed)
( )	Rope
( )	Clothes pins

Food List per Day per Person (3 alternatives per meal)

Breakfast	
	Instant oatmeal + dried fruit + almonds
	2 cups muesli/granola + ½ cup dried milk
	Freeze-dried scrambled eggs

Lunch	
	Canned, dried, smoked meat + crackers
	Fish in a pouch with 2 slices of bread
	Peanut butter (individ. cup) and 1.5oz crackers

Snacks	
	Nuts and seeds
	Dried fruit
	Protein/granola bars

Dinner	
	Freeze-dried instant meal
	1½ cups quinoa, dried veggies + broth
	2 cups pasta, dried tomatoes + herbs

Other Food Items / Condiments

	Sugar		Salt & pepper
	Coffee (and creamer)		Spices & herbs
	Powdered milk		Hot/soy sauce
	Tea		Vitamins & minerals
	Hot cider		Olive oil
	Powdered drink mixes		Chocolate, fruity sweets

Resupply

	Extra food rations		Celebratory treats
	Sunscreen (2oz/60g per week, min. SPF 30)		Clean clothing items (T-shirts, underwear, etc.)
	Toilet paper		Fresh fruit & veggies
	Condiments, spices, etc.		Extra batteries

! When packing your resupply package, keep in mind that you are not allowed to ship any flammable substances, including camp stove fuel.

G. Food Suggestions

Breakfast

- Instant oatmeal (purchase with or add flavors and sugar), porridge, semolina, and polenta with dried fruits
- Self-mixed cereals – with sesame, chia, flax, sunflower, pumpkin and other seeds; raisins and other dried fruit and berries; nuts; coconut flakes; rolled oats, shredded wheat, multi grains, etc.; mixed with dry milk, powdered soy, coconut, or almond milk, and possibly protein powder
- Pumpernickel (dark rye bread), tortilla, pita, or other dense, long-lasting breads
- Almond and peanut butter; tahini (sesame paste); chocolate spread; jelly and honey
- Freeze dried breakfasts, such as scrambled egg, hash brown, etc.
- Tea bags, tea pouches (such as ginger granulate), coffee, hot chocolate, sugar

Lunch

- Canned meat, smoked/dried sausage (e.g., traditional salami), beef and other jerkies
- Tuna and salmon in pouches; canned fish and mussels in sauces; dried salted fish and shrimp
- Hard-boiled eggs (for early trail days)
- Powdered hummus (add water and olive oil)
- Crackers or pita crisps (wheat, whole grain, quinoa, corn); breads and tortillas
- Vegemite, pouches of olive oil and herbs; other veggie/vegan spreads
- Aged cheeses (repackaged in breathable material keep rather well)

Snacks

- Almonds, pistachios, other nuts and seeds (no shells, with/-out flavors, smoked)
- Dried fruits (mango, apricot, banana, date, fig, apple, etc.) and berries; fruit leather
- Power bars and gels; protein, granola, and cereal bars; other candy and snack bars
- Sundried tomatoes, veggie chips, olives in oil
- Dried corn kernels for popcorn in the evening (refine with oil, salt, sugar)
- Chocolate, gummy bears, caramel bonbons (limit these “empty calories”)

Dinner

- Freeze-dried instant meals in pouches (try different varieties, flavors, and brands prior)
- Pasta with sundried tomatoes, tomato paste, and/or pesto, olive oil and spices, parmesan
- Quinoa, millet, and couscous with herbs and spices (and dried carrots, onion, peas)
- Soup base or stock cubes, add noodles or rice and flakes of mushroom, parsley, tomato, etc.
- Ramen noodles and other instant dishes (e.g., macaroni & cheese, dried mashed potatoes)
- Burritos with rice, chicken in a pouch, beans, cheese, dried bell pepper
- Mixed lentils, beans, and chickpeas with seasoning (mind the cooking times)
- Condiments: salt, spices, little sachets of mustard, ketchup, hot sauce, soy sauce, olive oil
- Herbal tea, instant hot chocolate, hot lemon with honey

H. Contact Information

General Questions & Permits

Yosemite Public Information Office

Mail: PO Box 577, Yosemite, CA 95389
Phone: +1 (209) 372-0200 (general); +1 (209) 372-0826 (permits)
Web: https://www.nps.gov/yose/planyourvisit/

Inyo National Forest

Mail: Inyo National Forest, 351 Pacu Lane, Ste 200, Bishop, CA 93514
Phone: +1 (760) 873-2400 (general); +1 (760) 873-2483 (permits)
Web: http://www.fs.usda.gov/main/inyo/passes-permits
http://www.recreation.gov (permits)

Devils Postpile National Monument

Mail: PO Box 3999, Mammoth Lakes, CA 93546
Phone: +1 (760) 934-2289
Web: https://www.nps.gov/depo/planyourvisit/
http://www.recreation.gov (permits)

Sierra National Forest

Mail: 1600 Tollhouse Road, Clovis, CA 93611
Phone: +1 (559) 297-0706
Web: http://www.fs.usda.gov/main/sierra/passes-permits

Sequoia & Kings Canyon National Park

Mail: 47050 Generals Highway, Three Rivers, CA 93271
Phone: +1 (559) 565-3341 (general); +1 (559) 565-3766 (permits)
Web: https://www.nps.gov/seki/planyourvisit/

Eastern Sierra Interagency Visitor Center (Mt. Whitney)

Mail: Highway 395 & CA-136, Lone Pine, CA 93545
Phone: +1 (760) 876-6200
Web: http://www.fs.usda.gov/recarea/inyo/recarea/?recid=20698

Lodging & Resupply Pickup

Red's Meadow Resort & Pack Station

Mail: PO Box 395, Mammoth Lakes, CA 93546
Phone: +1 (760) 934-2345
Web: http://www.redsmeadow.com/

Vermillion Valley Resort

Mail: 70000 Edison Lake Road, Mono Hot Springs, CA 93642
Phone: +1 (559) 259-4000
Web: http://www.edisonlake.com/

Muir Trail Ranch

Mail: PO Box 176, Lakeshore, CA 93634 (June to September)
PO Box 700, Ahwahnee, CA 93601 (October to May)
E-Mail: howdy@muirtrailranch.com
Web: http://www.muirtrailranch.com/

Mt. Williamson Motel and Base Camp

Mail: PO Box 128, 515 S Edwards St, Independence, CA 93526
Phone: +1 (760) 878-2121
Web: http://www.mtwilliamsonmotel.com

Yosemite Public Transit

YARTS (Yosemite Area Regional Transportation System)

Phone: +1 (877) 989-2787
Web: http://www.yarts.com

Glacier Point Bus

Phone: +1 (888) 413-8869
Web: http://www.travelyosemite.com/things-to-do/guided-bus-tours/

Resupply Delivery

Cottonwood Pack Station

Located 25 miles west of Lone Pine near Cottonwood and South Fork Lakes, serving the John Muir Wilderness.
Phone: +1 (760) 878-2015

Frontier Pack Train

Located in the June Lake Loop, serving the Ansel Adams Wilderness and Yosemite National Park.
Phone: +1 (760) 873-7971 (winter); +1 (760) 648-7701 (summer)

Mammoth Lakes Pack Outfit

Located in the Mammoth Lakes Basin, serving the John Muir Wilderness.
Phone: +1 (888) 475-8747
Web: http://www.mammothpack.com

McGee Creek Pack Station

Located 12 miles south of Mammoth Lakes, serving the John Muir Wilderness.
Phone: +1 (760) 878-2207 (winter); +1 (760) 935-4324 (summer)
Web: http://www.mcgeecreekpackstation.com

Red's Meadow Pack Train

Located near Devils Postpile National Monument, serving John Muir and Ansel Adams Wildernesses.
Phone: +1 (760) 934-2345 or +1 (800) 292-7758

Rock Creek Pack Station

Located in the Eastern Sierras between Mammoth Lakes and Bishop.
Phone: +1 (760) 873-8331
Web: http://www.rockcreekpackstation.com

Pack station information retrieved from:
www.fs.usda.gov/Internet/FSE_DOCUMENTS/stelprdb5176051.docx

I. Links & References

Online Resources

National Parks & U.S. Forest Services

The official National Park and U.S. Forest Service websites provide a wide range of essential information related to wildlife, vegetation and geology of a particular region, applicable wilderness regulations and permit procedures, accessibility of trails and current conditions, and many other relevant topics.

Yosemite (NPS/YOSE): *https://www.nps.gov/yose/*
Devils Postpile (NPS/DEPO): *https://www.nps.gov/depo/*
Sequoia & Kings Canyon (NPS/SEKI): *https://www.nps.gov/seki/*
Inyo National Forest: *http://www.fs.usda.gov/inyo/*
Sierra National Forest: *http://www.fs.usda.gov/sierra/*

Pacific Crest Trail Association

Dedicated to protect, preserve, and promote the 2,650-mile (4,265km) Pacific Crest Trail, the PCTA.org website also offers a variety of useful JMT thru-hike information, given the trail's significant overlap with the PCT.

Website: *http://www.pcta.org/*

Sierra Hikes

Comprehensive website that addresses various aspects of planning and preparing a thru-hike on the JMT. Very detailed exposition of the historic events that led to the construction of the trail as well as the different construction phases and parties involved.

Website: *http://jmt.sierra-hikes.com/*

Sierra Wild

Joint website of all agencies that manage wilderness areas along the Sierra Nevada that offers a wide array of information, such as trip planning, wilderness regulations, philosophy, current conditions, and much more.

Website: *http://www.sierrawild.gov/*

Recreation Equipment, Inc. (REI)

In addition to the large assortment of outdoor products, REI's website also offers practical expert advice and how-to explanations for popular outdoor activities, including hiking and backpacking.

Website: *https://www.rei.com/learn/expert-advice.html*

JMT Facebook & Yahoo Groups

With over 20,000 members, the JMT-specific Facebook and Yahoo groups represent a huge knowledge base that compiles a vast amount of first-hand advice and personal recommendations for every aspect of hiking the JMT. Seasoned JMT finishers gladly share their experience, and prospective hikers are welcome to ask any questions they may have.

Website: *Search for "John Muir Trail" on Facebook or Yahoo Groups*

SoCal Hiker Blog

SoCal Hiker's comprehensive JMT trip report contains detailed descriptions of individual trail sections, completed with lots of beautiful pictures and personal thru-hike impressions.

Website: *https://socalhiker.net/itinerary-for-the-john-muir-trail/*

Sierra Club Bulletin

Digitized version of the original Sierra Club Bulletin from February 1931. Many interesting anecdotes and insights into the organization of the Sierra Club at that time. Also contains a detailed account of how the "John Muir Memorial Rest Hut" (Muir Hut) was built.

Link: *https://archive.org/stream/sierraclubbullet161sier/*

Literature

Browning, P. (2011) *Sierra Nevada Place Names,* Wilderness Press

A great reference for those looking to learn more about how some of the places and features in the Sierra Nevada received their names.

Muir, J. (2013) *My First Summer in the Sierra: Illustrated Edition,* J Missouri

An updated edition of John Muir's original work, recounting his early travels in the Sierra Nevada while working as a shepherd in the summer of 1869. In his highly inspirational style, Muir describes the towering waterfalls, natural rock formations, and abundant plant and animal life, which ultimately helped him develop his views of the natural world.

Muir, J. (2014) *The Yosemite,* CreateSpace

This updated edition of John Muir's classic text contains timeless descriptions of Yosemite Valley's geography and the large variety of trees, flowers, birds, and other animals that can be found there.

Richins Jr., P. (2008) *Mt. Whitney: The Complete Trailhead to Summit Guide,* Mountaineers Books

A comprehensive guide to Mt. Whitney with useful information regarding best places to camp at on multi-day backpacking trips, interesting side trips, possible route variations, and "must-see" areas.

Schoenherr, A. A. (1992) *A Natural History of California (California Natural History Guides),* University of California Press

A comprehensive guide that describes the vegetation, wildlife, and geology of each distinctive region within the state of California.

Secor, R. J. (2009) *The High Sierra: Peaks, Passes, and Trails*, Mountaineers Books

A guide to the Sierra Mountains that details mountains and trails of Sierra high country, offering an extensive collection of side trips from the JMT.

Storer, T. I. (2004) *Sierra Nevada Natural History (California Natural History Guides),* University of California Press

A great all-around overview of the plants, animals, and topography of the Sierra Nevada, completed with interesting facts about its geological and human history.

Wallace, Z. (2016) *Plan & Go | High Sierra Trail,* Sandiburg Press

A comprehensive planning guide to hiking the 72-mile HST from the Giant Forest in Sequoia Nat'l Park to Whitney Portal at the base of Mt. Whitney.

Weeden, N. (1996) *A Sierra Nevada Flora,* Wilderness Press

A detailed guide to the flora of the Sierra Nevada that helps hikers identify wildflowers, ferns, shrubs, and trees in the field.

Documentaries

High Sierra – A Journey on the John Muir Trail (2012)

A first-hand experience along the John Muir Trail following a group of students as they make the 221-mile trek in the wake of John Muir's own footsteps. The film captures the visual splendor of the 'Range of Light' as well as the range of emotions and physical challenges that accompany such an adventure. The film also features Yosemite Park Ranger Shelton Johnson who shares insight about the trail and the meaning and importance of the American wilderness.

Watch for free at: *http://highsierradoc.com/*

Mile... Mile & a Half – The Muir Project (2013)

A feature-length documentary of five friends who leave their daily lives behind to hike California's historic John Muir Trail. Their goal – complete the journey in 25 days while capturing the amazing sights and sounds they encounter along the way. Inspired by their bond, humor, artistry, and dedication, the group continues to grow to include other artists, musicians, and adventure seekers. Before they all reach the summit of Mt. Whitney, hikers and viewers alike affirm the old adage – it's about the journey, not the destination.

Available for rent/purchase at: *http://themuirproject.com/*

And, of course, visit **www.PlanAndGoHiking.com** for more trail-specific information, pictures, and updates.

We look forward to and appreciate your feedback!

J. List of Abbreviations

CCW	Carrying a Concealed Weapon
DEPO	Devils Postpile National Monument
ETD	Estimate of Trail Days
FCFS	First-come, first-served
Mdw.	Meadow
MTR	Muir Trail Ranch
NF	National Forest
NOBO, NB	Northbound
NP	National Park
PLB	Personal Locator Beacon
RMR	Red's Meadow Resort
SEKI	Sequoia and Kings Canyon National Parks
SOBO, SB	Southbound
TH	Trailhead
TM	Tuolumne Meadows
UAS	Unmanned Aircraft System ("Drone")
USGS	United States Geological Survey
VVR	Vermillion Valley Resort
WP	Whitney Portal
YOSE	Yosemite National Park
YV	Yosemite Valley

About the Authors

Gerret was born 1981 in Hamburg, Germany. Since before he can remember, his father took him along on hikes and sparked his love of the outdoors. Gerret has since enjoyed hiking trips in various parts of the Alps, the Philippines, China, New Zealand, Canada, and the U.S. With his background in business and engineering, Gerret is always interested in improved gear and technical solutions. Besides the peace he feels when in nature, he enjoys the physical challenge the mountains pose.

Kevin is a seasoned backpacker who was first introduced to the fascinating world of hiking by his parents during family vacations in the beautiful Czech Giant Mountains and Saxon Elbe Sandstone Mountains in Eastern Europe. Inspired by those early adventures, Kevin went on to travel and explore Europe's largest mountain range, the Alps, on foot and on skis throughout the years. In 2011, he moved to San Diego, CA, which quickly became his gateway to United States' vast and varied backcountry. To Kevin, hiking is a great way to escape the comfort zone and reconnect with nature.

Special Thanks

I would especially like to thank:

My father, who introduced me to any sport I know how to play, investing much of his valued time. He also infected me with his passion for the mountains that he had developed as a child on various hikes with his father. In his smart but gentle manner, my father continues to be the supreme guidance in my life.

My friend Josh, who had the idea for this trip – just as he did for our first hitch-/ hiking trip in 1999 through southern Germany. Josh never ceases to amaze me with his unorthodox approaches at solving problems. He is equally goofy as well-educated. I am extremely thankful for his friendship.

My wife Nadja, who has always supported my travel and adventure plans, regardless of whether or not she could be a part of them. I admire her strength and intelligence, and am madly in love with her humor and beauty. I could not imagine a better companion with whom to journey through life.

My friend Kevin, who has been a trusted hiking buddy for many years. Our shared passion for the mountains and appreciation of nature have led to many memorable backpacking adventures. It was those experiences along with our long-time friendship that ultimately inspired the foundation of our own outdoor publishing company.

Disclaimer

The information provided in this book is accurate to the best of authors' and publisher's knowledge. However, there is no aspiration, guarantee, or claim to the correctness, completeness, and validity of any information given. Readers should be aware that internet addresses, phone numbers, mailing addresses, as well as prices, services, etc. were believed to be accurate at time of publication, but are subject to change without notice.

References are provided for informational purposes only. Neither authors nor the publisher have control over the content of websites, books, or other third party sources listed in this book and, consequently, do not accept responsibility for any content referred to herein. The mention of products, companies, organizations, or authorities in this book does not imply any affiliation with or endorsement by author(s) or publisher, and vice versa. All product and company names are trademarks™ or registered® trademarks of their respective holders.

This book is not a medical guidebook. The information and advice provided herein are merely intended as reference and explicitly not as a substitute for professional medical advice. Consult a physician to discuss whether or not your health and fitness level are appropriate for the physical activities describe in this book, especially, if you are aware of any pre-existing conditions or issues.

38992085R00108

Made in the USA
Middletown, DE
02 January 2017